LEARN SOME HANDS-ON HISTORY!

Amazing
Leonardo da Vinci
Inventions

YOU CAN BUILD
YOURSELF

MAXINE ANDERSON

nomad press

Nomad Press
A division of Nomad Communications
10 9 8 7 6 5 4 3 2 1
Copyright © 2006 by Nomad Press
ISBN: 0-9749344-2-9
Questions regarding the ordering of this book should be addressed to
Independent Publishers Group
814 N. Franklin St.
Chicago, IL 60610
www.ipgbook.com

Nomad Press
2456 Christian St.
White River Junction, VT 05001
www.nomadpress.net

Endorsements

"We are all living in a Renaissance. Ours is a technological Renaissance, which would have amazed Leonardo da Vinci. Although TV and the Internet have transformed our lives, many young people are losing touch with the vital hands-on skills of creativity and inventiveness. *Amazing Leonardo Inventions You Can Build Yourself* tackles this issue in a direct and inspiring way. Here is a book that encourages young readers to explore the genius of Leonardo in an interactive, hands-on way. By following Maxine Anderson's clear instructions, readers can develop confidence in their practical abilities, make some fascinating scientific discoveries, learn about one of the world's greatest geniuses, and have a huge amount of fun in the process."

—Laurence Anholt, Double Gold Award winners of the Smarties Book Prize and author of *Leonardo and the Flying Boy*

"Leonardo would be thrilled with this book! He taught his students the principle of DIMOSTRAZIONE— to think independently and learn through practical, hands-on experience. This is a wonderful resource for children, and for adults who wish to experience a Renaissance of their childlike love of learning."

—Michael J. Gelb, author of *How to Think Like Leonardo da Vinci*

"*Amazing Leonardo da Vinci Inventions You Can Build Yourself* is both fun and factual. Children will enjoy reading about his fascinating life and many creative and sometimes bizarre ideas, and be able to see his 'inventions' actually come to life."

—Robert Byrd, winner of The Golden Kite Award and author of *Leonardo: Beautiful Dreamer*

"Leonardo, whose name is synonymous with 'universal genius,' may well have possessed the most creative mind in history . . . Leonardo was also an astonishingly prescient scientist and engineer, who invented entire disciplines in science centuries before they were to be reinvented. *Amazing Leonardo da Vinci Inventions You Can Build Yourself* guides young readers to sample Leonardo's mind by replicating what were for him 'mental inventions.' The scheme cannot fail to make children more creative, more questioning, and more appreciative of nature as well as natural law."

—Bulent Atalay, PhD, scientist-artist and author of *Math and the Mona Lisa*

"A wonderful little book that gives an excellent introduction to Leonardo da Vinci, the quintessential Renaissance man. The text and illustrations are informative and engaging and surely will give kids a sense of Leonardo's great imaginative capacities as an artist, scientist, and inventor. The build yourself projects are both instructive and entertaining and very effectively make the past seem present. I think it is delightful."

—Joy Kenseth, PhD, Professor of Art History, Dartmouth College

"Leonardo da Vinci was the ultimate Renaissance person: a master artist, scientist, inventor, and dreamer. His ideas have fascinated scholars for centuries; many of his inventions bear an eerie resemblance to modern-day tools and machines. This marvelous book will introduce you to some of Leonardo's most exciting ideas and innovations. You'll also learn about the broader context in which Leonardo lived and worked. Best of all, you get to build machines and explore the world much like Leonardo himself did."

—David Kaiser, PhD, Physicist and Historian of Science, Massachusetts Institute of Technology

"Creative, curiosity-provoking, informational, and just plain fun—kids will find it irresistible."

—Rebecca Rupp, PhD, *Home Education Magazine*

Acknowledgments

Without the following people, this book would not have been possible. Many thanks to George Hart for his advice on Leonardo's polyhedra; Melinda Iverson of Brickfish Creative and the Leonardo Bridge Project for the use of the photograph of the Leonardo Bridge in Ås, Norway, as well as Leonardo's original sketch of the bridge; Jerry Everard for his design ideas for the helical airscrew; John Berkenkamp for his ideas and hands-on help creating the armoured tank; Lisa Spangenberg for her expertise on Renaissance Italy; Rafaella Panigada for her help contacting the right people at the right places in Italy; Robert Byrd, Laurence Anholt, Michael Gelb, Bulent Atalay, David Kaiser, Joy Kenseth, and Rebecca Rupp for their careful reviews and endorsements of the book; and to everyone at Nomad Press for their patience, skills, and good humor. It has been a pleasure to work with you.

Contents

Introduction

Have you ever had to do a chore that you just didn't want to do—and wished you could invent a machine to do it for you? Or wondered if you could build a flying machine, or a secret weapon, or invent something that no one had even considered before? That's what Leonardo da Vinci did, more than 500 years ago. Leonardo da Vinci is one of the world's best-known artists; he painted *Mona Lisa*, the world's most famous painting, and other very famous works of art. But Leonardo was also one of the most amazing and creative inventors ever to live. He filled hundreds of notebooks with ideas for inventions ranging from flying machines to armored tanks to shoes that could walk on water, and he did it at a time when people still believed that the earth was the center of the solar system and explorers still hadn't "discovered" the New World.

Leonardo's self-portrait at about age 60.

This book will help you discover Leonardo da Vinci, his life, ideas, and most importantly, his amazing inventions. You'll learn a little history of the time in which Leonardo lived, some interesting facts about the people and places around him, and also how to build working models of lots of Leonardo's inventions.

The book is divided into five main sections. **Leonardo the Artist and Dreamer** features Leonardo's inventions that focus on painting, drawing, drama, and other arts. **Leonardo's Useful Machines** cov-

A page from one of Leonardo's notebooks shows ideas for weapons.

ers inventions that Leonardo developed to make everyday life easier. **Leonardo and Water** explores Leonardo's obsession with the power of water and his quest to tame it, while **Leonardo in Flight** looks at some of the experiments Leonardo conducted in his quest to fly. **Leonardo's War Inventions** explores his inventions used for warfare.

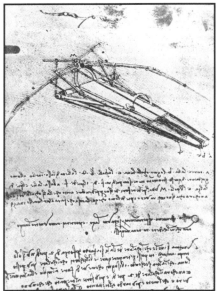

Most of the projects in this book can be made by kids without too much adult supervision, and most of the supplies for projects are probably already around your house. So, take a step back into Leonardo da Vinci's Renaissance and get ready to Build It Yourself.

Another page shows his design for a flying machine.

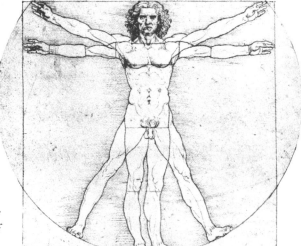

Perhaps one of the most famous images created by Leonardo, Vitruvian Man, *studies proportions of human anatomy.*

What Was the Renaissance?

When people talk about the time in world history called the Renaissance, they are talking about events that happened over a pretty big span of time. More than 250 years passed from the end of the Middle Ages in the 1300s to the beginning of the early Modern Age—and those 250 years are what historians today call the Renaissance.

But what was the Renaissance? The word renaissance means "rebirth" in French. In the late fourteenth, and throughout the fifteenth and sixteenth centuries, the countries of Europe went through a period of rebirth in culture, art, music, education, banking, politics, and industry that forever changed the way people lived, thought, and viewed the world.

During the thirteenth and most of the fourteenth century (from the 1200s to the 1350s), most of Europe was a feudal society. Kings owned huge tracts of land, and they gave big chunks of their land to nobles in exchange for the nobles' loyalty and protection in case of attack by enemies. The nobles, in turn, allowed peasants to live and work on their land. The peasants provided food and goods and services for the nobles and each other, in exchange for protection from invaders. For most people during this time, called the Middle Ages, life was simple, tough, and very isolated. Generations of people lived in the same small villages in which their grandfather's grandfather had been born, lived, and died, doing the same jobs or working the same trade as their ancestors. People rarely left their villages, because their only protection from warring armies was to stay close to home.

As the years passed, though, armies invaded each others' territories less and less, and village people began to move away from the places they had lived for generations. Over time, more and more people moved from feudal villages to the cities of Europe to make better lives for themselves. Cities offered people more opportunities to learn new or different trades than they could find in their home villages. But city life also meant crowded, unsanitary living conditions—perfect conditions for the spread of Black Death, the bubonic plague that wiped out more than a third of the entire population of Europe in the mid-1300s. The plague was almost always fatal, and it spread throughout the continent, hitting the cities hardest. So many people died from the plague that the entire continent of Europe went in an economic depression that lasted for decades. There were fewer people to buy and use what tradespeople were making and merchants were selling, and many families were poor. Lack of buyers meant that everyone, from suppliers to manufacturers to bankers, was affected.

Finally, the plague ran its course and populations began to increase throughout Europe. More people meant greater demand for goods and services, and the tradespeople and merchants, bankers and importers thrived, creating goods that they ex-

The Plague

Bubonic plague, or Black Death, first hit Italy in 1347. Within two months, almost half of the Italian population was dead. Several more bouts of the plague raced through Europe for the next several decades, and Italy lost three million people in a century. During the time Leonardo lived, in the late 1400s, the population of Italy was lower than it had been one hundred years earlier. Oddly enough, some historians believe that this was actually one reason that the Italian Renaissance was so successful: fewer people meant more food and more resources for those who lived during this time.

Understanding the Centuries

If you've ever wondered why the fifteenth century stands for the 1400s and not the 1500s—or, for that matter, why it's already the twenty-first century, even though we write the date with digits beginning with 20, look back to the first century, where this confusing trend began. Historians refer to the time since the birth of Jesus Christ as "the Common Era" and separate dates into "before the Common Era," or "BCE" and "Common Era," or "CE." Historians have dated the Common Era like this: since the first century began at Christ's birth, it started at year 0. Therefore the second century began at year 100 and is made up of all the years in the 100s (100–199). The third century includes all of the years in the 200s and so on. Any guesses as to which hundred years the twenty-third century will include?

changed with merchants and suppliers in other countries throughout the world.

In fact, business was so good that a new class of people emerged who not only had enough money for all the daily necessities of life, like food and clothing, but had money to spare—money they wanted to spend on things like fancy houses, beautiful clothes, lovely paintings and artwork, and exotic food. This new middle class also was interested in education: bankers needed to be good at arithmetic, merchants needed to be able to read and communicate in foreign languages, and many wanted to learn for learning's sake alone. This new middle class didn't have to work from sunup to sundown just to survive. They had free time, and they used it to learn about art, music, language, science, and politics.

Part of the reason this time in history is called the "rebirth," or Renaissance, is that many classical ideas about learning and the arts from ancient Greece and Rome were revived. The ancient Greeks and Romans had focused on human achievement rather than the glorification of God, but in the centuries just before the Renaissance (the Middle Ages), most art and writing in Europe focused on God. People didn't look outward at the world, but rather upward to the heavens. During the Renaissance people rediscovered the Greek and Roman languages, ancient literature, and classical ideals, and

Art in the Renaissance

For artists, the Renaissance was a time that changed both the style of art and the purpose of art. In Europe during the Middle Ages, art was used to glorify God: paintings and sculptures were created for religious purposes, to be placed in churches and chapels and offered as a tribute from humankind to God. During the Renaissance, artists shifted their focus from works of art glorifying God to works of art exploring humankind's relationship to God and to each other. For the first time, religious figures were portrayed as real people in real settings.

Greek and Roman scholars taught the classical ideals of ancient Greece to the new middle class of Italians eager to learn. Because Italy was ideally situated as a trading center between Byzantium and the ancient empires in the east and Europe in the west, many of its coastal cities became centers for trade, wealth, culture, and education.

One of these cities was Florence, the city where Leonardo da Vinci spent much of his youth. Unlike some other cities in Italy, which were ruled by the Catholic church or by noble families, Florence was ruled by the Medicis, a family of merchants who became wealthy and powerful through their business success, rather than by birth.

The Medicis were patrons of the arts and education: they loved beautiful art and entertainment and supported learning and discovery in many different fields.

Wealthy, powerful families in other Italian cities also supported artists and scientists, teachers, and dreamers in their quest for classical learning. This support led to scientific discoveries, new kinds of art and architecture, and even the exploration of the New World.

patron—a supporter

Tomb of Giuliano dé Medici designed and sculpted by Michelangelo.

Biography of Leonardo

Leonardo da Vinci was born on April 15, 1452, in Vinci, Italy, just outside of Florence. Leonardo's father and mother weren't married, and Leonardo spent most of his childhood with his father, while his mother lived in a neighboring town. His mother and father both married other people, and Leonardo ended up with 17 half brothers and sisters.

Leonardo showed enormous talent as an artist early on, and when he was 15, his father arranged for him to become an apprentice in the workshop of Andrea del Verrocchio, one of the most well-known artists in Florence. Leonardo stayed with Verrocchio for almost 10 years, learning about all aspects of the artist's trade, including sculpture, goldsmithing, painting, and metal casting. During his time as an apprentice, Leonardo helped Verrocchio create some of his most famous works, including the copper ball on top of the giant cupola of the Duomo of Santa Maria del Fiore, the famous cathedral in Florence, and the painting, *The Baptism of Christ*.

Leonardo finished his apprenticeship under Verrocchio and in 1477 went to work on his own. His first patron was the duke of Milan, Ludovico Sforza. Leonardo began working for Sforza in 1482 and continued to work for him for the next 17 years. The patronage ended when Sforza was forced out of power in 1499. During the years Leonardo worked for the duke, he not only created some of his most famous paintings, but also designed pageants, stage sets, costumes, weapons, buildings, and machinery.

Leonardo filled more than 100 notebooks with his ideas. The notebooks included designs for a perfect city, machines that would make everyday work easier and more efficient, weapons that could be used against an invading army, vehicles that could

What's in a Name?

Most famous people in history are referred to by their last name: Abraham Lincoln is referred to as "Lincoln," not "Abraham," for example, and Winston Churchill is referred to as "Churchill," not "Winston." But Leonardo da Vinci has always been referred to as "Leonardo," not "da Vinci." Why? Unlike today, where we are given our first names and inherit our last names, during the Renaissance, people were given only a first name when they were born. Their last name, if they took one, usually referred to where they were born: Leonardo was born in Vinci, Italy, and his name means, "Leonardo from Vinci." Other last names identified what someone did for a living (Thomas Shoemaker) or who their father was (Giovanni di Paolo, for example, means "Giovanni, son of Paolo"). Sometimes people were identified by what they looked like—the color of their hair, for instance, or the shape of their nose. ("Massacio" means "Big Thomas," for example.) If you were alive during the Renaissance, what last name would you use?

fly, and theories about mathematics, optics, and painting. He also spent years studying and drawing human and animal anatomy.

The one thing that Leonardo lacked was an ability to settle down and finish his projects. Of all the projects he started in the 17 years he worked for the duke of Milan, he only finished six of them. One of his most famous works, *The Last Supper*, took several years to finish and when Leonardo finally completed it, the painting began to disintegrate almost immediately because he used an experimental painting technique that didn't work.

After the French invaded Italy in 1499 and Ludovico Sforza fell from power, Leonardo traveled throughout Italy for 17 years, working for several powerful rulers, including a brutal military leader named Cesare Borgia, Pope Leo X, and the Medici family. One of the most interesting projects Leonardo worked on during this time was the *Bridge of the Golden Horn*, a design for

The Last Supper.

a bridge over 700 feet long that would cross the harbor of Istanbul in the Ottoman Empire, which is now Turkey. The design called for a bridge 72 feet wide and 120 feet above sea level at the highest point of the span. Leonardo's bridge was never built, and it wasn't until the 1850s that a bridge was built on Leonardo's proposed site.

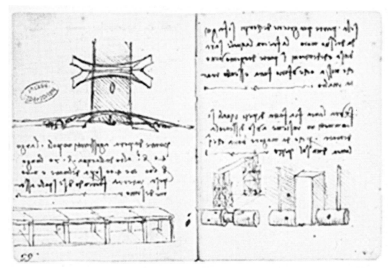

Design for the Bridge of the Golden Horn *from one of Leonardo's notebooks.*

In 1503 Leonardo started working on his most famous painting, *Mona Lisa* (known in Italy and other places in Europe as *La Gioconda*, "the laughing woman"). For a long time experts disagreed on who Mona Lisa was, or whether Leonardo was hired to paint her, but today most scholars agree that Mona Lisa was the wife of an important man in Florence, named Francesco del Giocondo. It was one of the few paintings that Leonardo finished and kept for himself, so it must have been very important to him.

In 1516, the king of France offered Leonardo a job as the "premier painter and engineer and architect of the king." Leonardo accepted the job and went to live near the king in a lovely house in Amboise, France. Leonardo was in his sixties and quite ill and weak, but he loved living in France, and he and King Francis became very close. Leonardo was paralyzed on his right side, but still drew every day, working on sketches and designing inventions.

Leonardo died on May 2, 1519. He was 67 years old. Some historians say that King Francis was at Leonardo's side, cradling his head in his arms when he died.

timeline

April 14, 1452: Leonardo da Vinci is born in Vinci, near Florence

1467–1477: Leonardo goes to Florence to work as an apprentice under the famous artist Andrea del Verrochio, learning everything about the artist's trade. Leonardo probably helped design the machinery to put the 2-ton copper ball that was placed on the top of the dome of the Cathedral of Santa Maria del Fiore.

1482–1499: Leonardo goes to work for Ludovico Sforza, the Duke of Milan, as his military engineer. Leonardo creates paintings, designs costumes, and fills his notebooks with ideas and drawings about nature, science, hydraulics, mechanics of inventions, and machines. This eventually results in nearly 4,000 pages of sketches and notes.

1490s: Leonardo writes his theory on the flight of birds and draws many sketches of machines designed to mimic bird flight. Leonardo may have tried out some of his flying machine ideas.

1495–1498: Leonardo paints *The Last Supper* using a new technique of oil and varnish on dry plaster. Unfortunately, the experiment was a disaster and the painting began to disintegrate almost immediately.

1499: The French invade Milan and Ludovico Sforza falls from power, leaving Leonardo unemployed and without a source of income.

1502: Leonardo works for Cesare Borgia as a mapmaker and military engineer.

1503: Leonardo begins to paint *Mona Lisa*.

1506: Leonardo leaves Florence for Milan, where he studies anatomy, creating anatomical sketches so accurate they are used by medical students for several hundred years.

1509: *The Divine Proportion,* a book on mathematical proportion written by Luca Pacioli and illustrated by Leonardo, is published. It is the first book on geometric proportion with illustrations and becomes the standard text on the subject for many years to come.

1513–1516: Leonardo works for the Pope in Rome. The Pope forbids him to dissect cadavers (humans after they've died), which is important to his study of anatomy.

1515: Leonardo paints his last painting, *St. John the Baptist,* which today hangs in the Louvre Museum, in Paris.

1516: Leonardo is hired by King Francis as a member of his court, and moves to France.

1519: Leonardo dies in Cloux, France, and is buried in Amboise.

Leonardo the Artist and Dreamer

Leonardo is one of the world's most famous artists, and his paintings are the most studied and analyzed in the history of art, even though only a few of his works survive.

Leonardo began drawing when he was a child growing up in Florence and showed talent early. In fact, his father was so impressed with Leonardo's drawing ability that when Leonardo was in his early teens, his father brought some of Leonardo's drawings to the well-known artist Andrea del Verrocchio. Verrocchio must have been impressed, because he invited Leonardo to become an apprentice in his *bottega*, or artists' studio.

Mona Lisa, one of Leonardo's greatest achievements.

During the Renaissance, being an artist was a trade, similar to being a blacksmith, weaver, or other craftsperson. Unlike today's artists, who usually create a work of art by themselves from start to finish and who usually specialize in just one medium, such as painting or sculpture, artists in the Renaissance worked together on projects, with different artists working on different parts of a project at any given time. Artists often worked equally well in many different media. For example, if Verrocchio were offered a job to paint a portrait for a church, several of the artists in his studio would work

Andrea del Verrocchio (1435–1488)

When Leonardo was apprenticed to Andrea del Verrocchio, he was being taken under the wing of one of the most influential artists of his time. Andrea del Verrocchio was a gifted goldsmith as well as a painter and sculptor. In his studio he trained Botticelli, another very famous painter, and also worked with Michelangelo. While most of his paintings have been lost to history, Verrocchios's most famous sculpture still stands in Venice, Italy. It is a bronze sculpture of a famous Venetian soldier named Bartolomeo Colleoni. What makes this statue so remarkable is that it was the first time a sculptor had created a statue of a horse with one of the legs in a raised position—the entire weight of the statue is carried on three legs rather than four, a very difficult accomplishment.

Andrea del Verrocchio

on parts of the painting. If he received a commission to create a sculpture, the same artists might work together on that. *bottega—artist's studio*

One of the earliest examples of Leonardo's work, in fact, is in a painting called *The Baptism of Christ,* that was created in Verrocchio's studio. Leonardo painted one of the angels, as well as the background of this painting, and the story goes that when Verrocchio saw Leonardo's work, he was so overcome by his pupil's talents that he decided to stop painting. The story probably isn't true, but it suggests how unusually talented Leonardo was as an artist.

Leonardo spent much of his time drawing. He carried a notebook with him at all times, tied to a thong around his waist, and he would often stop to sketch what he saw around him, whether it was a group of old men laughing in a town square or a flock of swallows in flight. This practice made him very aware of how people and animals moved, and he captured this movement in his paintings. He was the first artist to study the physical

The Baptism of Christ—*Leonardo painted the angel to the far left, as well as the background.*

proportions of people, and he used this knowledge to create accurately pro-portioned figures in his paintings.

Leonardo also perfected the technique of chiar-oscuro, using light and dark (or shadow) to make his figures look three-dimensional. Another tech-nique, called sfumato (literally, "smoky"), blurred forms to create the illusion of distance in the background. It was first developed by Flemish and Venetian painters, but Leonardo perfected it to make his figures in the foreground seem soft and gentle. He used sfumato to create some of his most famous masterpieces, including *Mona Lisa*.

One of the things that set Leonardo apart from artists who came before him was that Leonardo cre-ated his paintings to tell a story—not just a scene from a story, but the entire story. This was a totally new concept in art, and he was a master at it. As one historian said, Leonardo's paintings are "silent poetry."

From Leonardo's Notebooks

"... If you open your legs so much as to decrease your height by ¹⁄₁₄ and spread and raise your arms till your middle fingers touch the level of the top of your head you must know that the centre of the outspread limbs will be the navel and the space between the legs will be an equilateral triangle.
... The length of a man's outspread arms is equal to his height ... from the bottom of [a man's] chin to the top of his head is one eighth of his height."

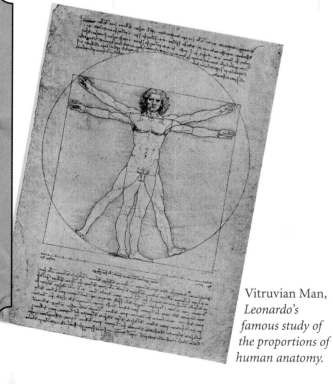

Vitruvian Man, *Leonardo's famous study of the proportions of human anatomy.*

Perspective and Leonardo's "Perspectograph"

One of the most interesting and important changes in art that occurred during the Renaissance was the discovery of an idea that made it possible for painters to translate the three-dimensional world they lived in onto the two-dimensional surface of a painting. This idea is called "linear perspective."

Linear perspective was first invented by a famous Renaissance architect named Filippo Brunelleschi, who had a system that helped show how objects shrink in size according to their distance from the eye. Brunelleschi's system has been lost

Filippo Brunelleschi (1377–1446)

Filippo Brunelleschi was trained as a sculptor and was also a goldsmith, mathematician, engineer, and inventor, but he was most famous as an architect. Brunelleschi designed the dome that covers the Basilica of Santa Maria del Fiore in Florence, Italy, which, when it was finally completed in 1434, became the first large-scale dome built in Italy since ancient times. Brunelleschi designed his dome to be built from spiraling rows of bricks forming two light shells, so it wouldn't need a scaffolding framework. The result was a symmetrical dome, or cupola, consisting of eight brick faces reaching 91 meters high. The construction of the Duomo, as it was called, took most of Brunelleschi's life. When it was finally completed, the dome was topped by a lantern with a copper sphere on top, cast in Andrea del Verrocchio's studio and raised to the top of the cupola by machines designed by del Verrocchio's apprentice, Leonardo.

Linear Perspective

The basic idea behind linear perspective is actually pretty simple: in every painting an artist creates a "floor" or area of the painting where the figures and/or objects will be placed. The floor ends at a horizon line, and the horizon line has a vanishing point on it. The artist then draws parallel lines radiating from the vanishing point outward. Images closest to the vanishing point should appear smaller and closer together, and images farthest from the vanishing point should appear larger and farther apart, giving the impression of depth and space in the painting.

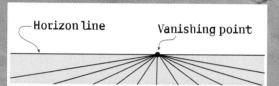

to history, but in 1435, a painter and architect named Leon Battista Alberti wrote a book called *On Painting*, in which he described a method that painters could use that would actually do just what Brunelleschi suggested: make what was painted on the canvas look three-dimensional.

Alberti's book had a huge influence on painters during the Renaissance, including Leonardo. He learned about Alberti's theory of linear perspective during his days as an apprentice in Verrocchio's studio, and all of Leonardo's paintings, even his early ones, show that he not only understood linear perspective, he took the idea of perspective even further.

Leonardo considered a painting a window to the outside world, and wanted everything in his paintings to look as if it were a scene through a window, happening before the viewer's eyes. Because he was a careful observer of nature, he noticed that at different times of day objects in the distance looked more or less sharp and took on

Leonardo's angel against the background in The Baptism of Christ

slightly different colors. Other painters had also noticed this and even had started showing it in their paintings, but Leonardo carefully measured and recorded what he noticed. For example, Leonardo noticed that in the morning light, distant objects (such as hills or mountains) looked less distinct and more blue than closer hills or mountains. He also noticed that the farther away the image was, the more its color blended into the color of the air around it.

As a result of his observations, Leonardo came up with some simple rules for painters to follow in creating what he called aerial perspective: the nearest object should be painted its true color, the one immediately behind the nearest one should be painted proportionately bluer, and the object farther away should be proportionately bluer still.

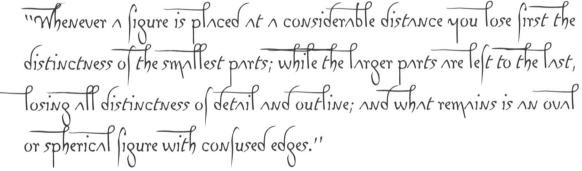

"Whenever a figure is placed at a considerable distance you lose first the distinctness of the smallest parts; while the larger parts are left to the last, losing all distinctness of detail and outline; and what remains is an oval or spherical figure with confused edges."

In addition to laying out rules for aerial perspective, Leonardo thought long and hard about how to create a machine for sketching a scene with the proper linear perspective. This machine he invented was called a perspectograph, and it helped artists design a replica of the scene they wanted to paint in proper perspective.

Leonardo's perspectograph was simply a clear pane of glass placed into a frame that held a small viewing slot. The painter put the pane of glass in the frame, placed the perspectograph in front of the scene to be painted, and then looked through the viewing slot with one eye and sketched the outline of the scene onto the glass. The artist could then transfer the rough sketch onto canvas as an outline and paint in the details.

Artists since Leonardo have created many different versions of the perspectograph, including ones with grids that made it really easy to transfer a rough sketch onto a piece of paper or canvas: an artist would simply have to draw whatever lines appeared on any given grid number, and the complete picture would come together.

Build It Yourself

Build Your Own Perspectograph

What you'll need

- heavy cardboard for frame—an old pizza box works well
- CD case broken apart into top and bottom pieces
- ruler
- Xacto knife
- dry-erase marker
- tracing paper
- sheets of acetate—clear plastic often used for overhead projectors

What to do

1 Draw and cut out templates A and B from the cardboard.

2 Measure the length of the CD case and cut a slot into template A so the CD cover fits in snugly.

3 Measure the length of your eyepiece (template B) and cut another slot in template A so the eyepiece fits snugly.

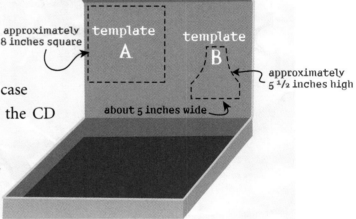

approximately 8 inches square

template A

template B

approximately 5 ½ inches high

about 5 inches wide

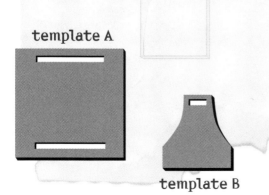

Clear top to CD case

template A

template B

4 Cut a slot in the narrow end of the eyepiece so you can see out of it with one eye. Make sure when you look through the eyepiece that you look through the CD case to the scene you want to draw. If the eyepiece is too high, cut some off the bottom of the template until you can see through the CD case when you look through the eyepiece slot.

5 Look through your perspectograph and trace the outline of the scene onto the CD case with the dry erase marker. Then remove the CD case from the frame—you will have a small but accurate outline of the scene!

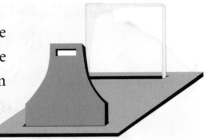

Alternative method for a larger drawing:

Remove the CD case from your perspectograph. Move to a large window. Tape a sheet of acetate (clear plastic) onto the window, and line up the perspectograph with the acetate so when you look through the eyepiece the acetate is between you and the scene you want to sketch. Draw the outline of the scene you see through the eyepiece onto the acetate, then transfer it to a sheet of tracing paper.

Draw One- and Two-Point Perspective

The idea of creating linear perspective in a drawing may seem tricky, but it's actually really easy. Here's how it's done:

What you'll need
- paper, several pieces
- pencil, with a good eraser and sharp tip
- dark-colored pencil or pen
- ruler

What to do

One-point perspective:

1 With your paper lengthwise, use your ruler to draw a horizontal line across the paper about one-third of the way down. This line is called the horizon. Make a dot roughly in the center of this line. This spot is called your vanishing point.

2 Next, draw a rectangle about two thirds of the way down the page. Make sure that the box is roughly in the center of the page.

3 From the top two corners of the rectangle, draw light, straight lines to the vanishing point. These lines are called orthogonals, or vanishing lines.

4 Draw a horizontal line somewhere between these two orthogonals. Darken this horizontal line as well as the orthogonal lines connecting this line to the box. Erase the orthogonal lines between the top of the box

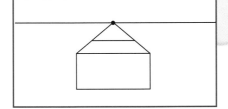

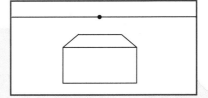

and the vanishing point. Now, do you see a three-dimensional box?

5 For another perspective, draw a square or rectangle to the right of the vanishing point.

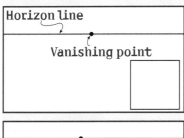

Horizon line

Vanishing point

6 Draw three orthogonal lines to the vanishing point this time—one from the top two corners of the square or rectangle and the third from the bottom left corner of the square or rectangle.

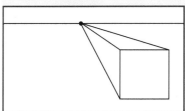

7 Draw a horizontal line between the top two orthogonal lines (the lines from the top two corners of the square). Darken this line and the orthogonal lines connecting it to the two corners of the box.

8 Next, drop a vertical line from the middle orthogonal line to the bottom orthogonal line. You should now see the side of the box forming.

9 Darken the lines that connect the dimensions of the box. You should see a box front, side, and top in this image. Erase the orthogonal lines connecting the box to the vanishing point.

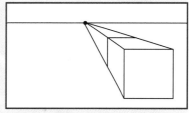

10 You can experiment with different placements of your square and rectangle and see what kinds of box shapes and perspectives you get.

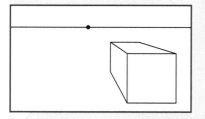

perspective—three-dimensional into two-dimensional

Two-point perspective:

1 Using your ruler, start by drawing the same horizon line, about one-third of the way down the page.

2 Draw vanishing points near each end of the horizon line. Label the points V1 and V2.

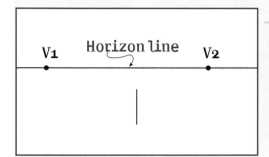

3 About two-thirds of the way down the paper, draw a short (2-inch) vertical line. This should be approximately in the center of the two vanishing points.

4 Using your ruler, draw lines from the top of the vertical line to each vanishing point, and from the bottom of the vertical line to each vanishing point. You should now have four orthogonal lines, two from the top of the vertical line and two from the bottom.

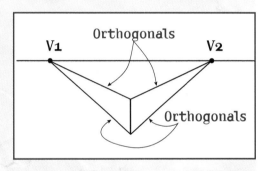

5 Draw vertical lines between each of the two orthogonal lines.

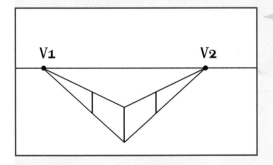

6 From the top and bottom of these vertical lines, draw orthogonal lines to the opposite vanishing point. This means that the vertical line on the left will have orthogonal lines to V2, while the vertical line on the right will have orthogonal lines to V1.

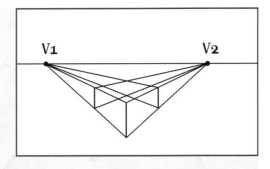

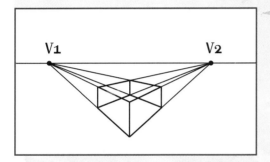

7 These four orthogonal lines have two intersections right above the first vertical line you drew. Draw a vertical line between these two intersections.

8 Darken the lines that connect the four vertical lines. You should end up with a picture of a three-dimensional box, in which you can see all sides of the box. Erase the orthogonal lines between your box and the vanishing points.

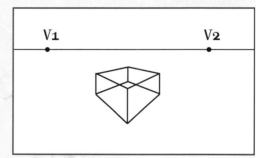

Before Linear Perspective

Before the Renaissance, artists didn't creating paintings in perspective. In fact, most paintings in the Middle Ages didn't have background images at all. Backgrounds were painted solid colors, very often gold. Why? Most European art in the time before the Renaissance showed religious figures such as Christ, and since none of the painters had seen heaven, they often painted the backgrounds gold, believing that the air in heaven must be very precious.

Masks for a Masque

One of Leonardo's many talents was performing. He played the lute and sang beautifully, loved playing practical jokes and telling riddles, and was often asked to perform for his friends in the evenings. When Leonardo had his own *bottega* in Milan during the 1490s, it was often crowded with friends, fellow artists, and musicians. In fact, it's said that when he was painting his most famous work, *Mona Lisa*, Leonardo hired clowns, jugglers, and musicians to come to the studio to make his model for the painting smile. This story may or may not be true, but there is no doubt that Leonardo loved to entertain and be surrounded by entertainment.

He wasn't alone. The Renaissance was a time of elaborate pageants and festivals, especially in the large cities, often held to celebrate special occasions in honor of the ruling families. Leonardo created costumes and stage sets for many celebrations. Because he was so skilled at making lifelike figures, he was especially good at making masks, which were often worn at parades, festivals, parties, and balls.

While many of the masks he made were beautiful, Leonardo also created masks that were grotesque, and some that were downright scary. For one pageant, Leonardo created a mask with a helmet that had spiraled horns, a serpent sticking out of the top, and a

Sketches for masks by Leonardo—when turned upside down, the dog in the upper left becomes a bat.

dragon's tail trailing down the wearer's back. It was supposed to look like a dragon sitting on top of his head. Some of Leonardo's masks were jokes, such as the mask he made of an elephant head playing its own trunk like a clarinet. Others were wearable optical illusions: Leonardo designed one mask that looked like a strange kind of dog—but when the mask was turned upside down, it looked a lot like a bat.

Il Paradiso: The Paradise Pageant

Leonardo wasn't only a great mask maker, he was also a terrific set designer. In 1490, Leonardo helped present a pageant to celebrate the marriage of the Duke of Milan's nephew to Isabella of Aragon, a woman who was said to be so beautiful, she "seemed like a sun."

The pageant was called Il Paradiso *(Paradise), and took place on a stage designed by Leonardo with actors costumed as the seven (known) planets orbiting the stage, reciting poetry that praised Isabella's beauty. The poetry wasn't especially memorable, but Leonardo's stage set and the costumes he designed have been remembered and commented on for centuries. Leonardo created the stage in the shape of an egg and covered it in gold. He placed lights behind glass to make them brighter and seem to glow. Around the top of the stage, he created a hidden system of pulleys and levers, so that the twelve signs of the zodiac moved around their orbits, almost as if by magic. Parts of the set were attached to winches hidden underneath the stage, that were rotated by unseen members of the production—making it appear to the audience that the scenery was moving itself.*

Sketches of a costume for a theatrical performance.

Build It Yourself

Make a Leonardo Masque Mask

What you'll need
- gallon-size milk jug
- scissors or an Xacto knife
- permanent marker
- manila folder or card stock for horns or ears, and tape
- bucket or bowl to mix and hold the papier-mâché
- unbleached flour, water, salt
- old newspaper
- paint and paintbrush
- glue and decorating materials like buttons, feathers, glitter, yarn for hair
- elastic and stapler

What to do

1 Cut the jug in half at the seam; use either side to make a mask, but the handle makes a good nose shape.

2 Mark on the jug with a permanent marker where you want the eyes to be. If you're using the side with the handle, putting eyes on either side of the handle creates a face-like image—the handle will look like a nose, with the top of the milk jug pointing toward the floor.

3 If you want to make horns for your mask, roll two pieces of card stock or other stiff, rugged paper into cones and tape them securely onto the front of the milk jug. Papier-mâché is heavy and will crush cones made from regular paper.

4 Create the papier-mâché paste by mixing one cup of flour, a little bit of salt, and two cups of warm water. The mix should have a consistency a little bit thinner than white glue.

5 Cut or tear newspaper into strips about 1 inch wide by 6 inches long. Cut up more than you think you'll need (which is a lot), because once you start dipping the strips into the paste you'll be up to your elbows in goop. If you don't have enough newspaper, you can use brown paper towels or even magazines, although they tend to be very slippery and don't hold the paste as well.

6 Start the process by dipping the newspaper into the papier-mâché paste. Do the back of the mask first if you want to paint or decorate that side. Work in one direction, and make sure that all the milk jug surfaces get covered by at least one layer of paper.

7 Move to the front of the mask, making sure to cover all surfaces. You can cover any other additions you've taped onto the front by wrapping pieces of newspaper around them and smoothing them over. Make the surface as smooth as possible, and wipe off excess papier-mâché goop. Put the mask in a safe place to dry, for about 24 hours.

8 When it is completely dry, paint the entire mask any color you'd like. White will cover up the newspaper and you can paint color on top of it.

9 Allow the paint to dry, and then add other decorations—feathers, yarn, fake flowers, glitter . . . Use your imagination and be creative!

10 Allow the entire mask to dry thoroughly again. In order to wear the mask, cut a piece of elastic long enough to go around the back of your head, with some extra to attach to the mask. Staple the elastic to your mask, about halfway up the jug.

"Plastic Glass" and Paint

If you were a painter in the Renaissance, you wouldn't be able to run to the hobby shop to pick up a couple tubes of oil paint or grab your watercolor kit out of the craft cupboard. During the Renaissance, artists made all of their own paints, turning many into very skilled chemists.

Most artists in the early 1500s painted with tempera paints on wood panels. Tempera is a fast-drying paint made from a combination of egg yolks and other ingredients that have been ground into a fine powder. Different ingredients made different colors. Shades of yellow, for example, could be made by grinding down crocuses, the stamens of lilies, or even saffron, a bright yellow spice. Ultramarine blue, a very bright blue often seen in Renaissance paintings, was made by grind-

The Last Supper *began deteriorating soon after Leonardo completed it.*

Egg Tempera vs. Oil Paint

Egg tempera is made by mixing colored pigments with egg yolk; the egg yolk acts as a binding agent, which keeps the color on the surface of the board, plaster, or canvas—whatever the painter happens to be painting on. Egg tempera had some major limitations for renaissance painters. It couldn't be stored, so painters had to make it immediately before they used it. Artists also had to be careful to make just the right amount of paint: too little and they'd have to try to match the color they had just run out of; too much and they'd waste expensive material. Because egg tempera dried very quickly, painters layered wet colors over dry colors to give the impression of shading and blending rather than mix colors together.

Egg tempera's limitations didn't bother painters in the Middle Ages. The religious figures they painted weren't supposed to look especially realistic—the figures were meant to represent saints and holy people, and so did not have to be to life-like. During the Renaissance, though, painters wanted to paint the world around them. They needed to show the natural world in a more realistic way. Luckily, oil paints enabled them to do this.

Oil paints were used as early as the twelfth century in northern Europe, but it wasn't until the fifteenth century that painters in the Netherlands began using oil paints to show incredibly realistic scenes in bold, vivid colors. Since oil paint dried very slowly, it could be stored for extended periods of time. Painters could take their time, and mix and blend colors to get shades they had never been able to achieve with egg tempera. The oil made the pigment in the paint translucent, so artists could paint very thin layers, giving their paintings a depth and inner glow that had never been seen before.

ing a precious stone called lapis lazuli. Purple could be made from ground mollusk shells.

What set Leonardo apart from most other artists of his time was his constant experimenting with different kinds of material to use for paint. He was one of the first Italian artists to use oil paints—invented by painters from the Netherlands—rather than egg tempera.

The problem was that Leonardo the Scientist often prevented Leonardo the Artist from successfully finishing his work. Leonardo often painted with experimental mixtures of materials that didn't work especially well, or tried new combinations of paints and painting surfaces with sometimes disastrous results. Leonardo painted his famous masterpiece, *The Last Supper*, on the wall of the monastery of Santa Maria delle Grazie, which had plaster walls. Instead of using egg tempera on a wet plaster base, which is what had been used very success- fully for centuries, Leonardo used tempera on dry plaster so he could work more slowly. He first treated the plaster with a varnish to seal it against moisture, but the varnish re- acted badly with the acid and salt in the walls of the church. The plaster began to chip and flake off the wall almost immediately, and only a few years after Leonardo finished the painting, it had already deterioriated badly. Today, even after centuries of attempt- ed restoration, many parts of *The Last Supper* are lost forever.

> The problem was that Leonardo the Scientist often prevented Leonardo the Artist from successfully finishing his work.

But what was great about Leonardo was that many of the experiments he conducted for one reason ended up resulting in something totally new and completely unexpected. That is how he invented the very first plastic. One day, Leonardo boiled together glue, eggs, vegetable dyes, saffron, poppy dust, and whole lilies (among other things), and created a mixture that hardened into what he described as "plastic glass." Leonardo painted different surfaces with many layers of his mixture and discovered that when the mixture dried, it could be carved into useful objects such as chess pieces, knife handles, candleholders, and salt shakers.

For centuries the recipe for Leonardo's plastic glass was lost to history, but in 2004 an Italian scholar searching through Leonardo's writings discovered all of the ingredients Leonardo used to create his plastic glass—and it worked! Alessandro Vezzosi followed Leonardo's recipe and painted cabbage and lettuce leaves, paper, and even ox intestines, just like Leonardo did 400 years before. When the mixture dried, it turned to Leonardo's "plastic glass."

Build It Yourself

Make Your Own Plastic

While this recipe doesn't involve boiling lilies or eggs, combining the following ingredients over heat will result in a natural plastic that you can shape, dry, carve, and paint, very similar to Leonardo's plastic glass.

What you'll need
- ½ cup heavy cream
- up to ½ cup white vinegar

What to do

1 Pour the cream into a saucepan and heat. Do not let it boil.

2 When it starts to simmer, stir in two spoonfuls of vinegar. Slowly simmer over medium heat. You will start to see yellowish lumps (curds) forming. These curds are a mixture of fat, minerals, and the protein casein (a natural plastic).

3 Keep adding vinegar and stirring until the liquid turns mostly to curds. Take it off the heat, let it cool, then strain the liquid from the casein curds and rinse the curds in cool water.

4 Knead the curds until they stick together and have the consistency of a ball of dough. Then shape it any way you like and let it dry overnight.

Build It Yourself

Make Your Own Paint

What you'll need

- dirt and two rocks
- egg yolk
- brush
- painting surface

pigment from ground-up dirt **+** egg yolk **=** paint

What to do

1 Here's an easy way to make your own paint. Go outside and find some interesting colored dirt, or even a crumbly piece of brick. Scoop up a little, let it dry overnight, and then crush the dirt between two rocks so it's powdery.

2 Mix the dirt with some egg yolk, and paint it on a piece of paper, a board, or even a flat rock. Try experimenting with dirt taken from different locations—you'll be surprised at the variety of colors plain old dirt can have.

3 Try other ingredients: the pistils or stamens of daylilies, for example, will make a bright yellow paint, as will crumbled saffron. Charcoal will make a grayish black paint. Experiment with natural ingredients you can find around your house, yard, or park. Just remember that in order to work well, they need to be crushed to a fine powder, then mixed with the egg yolk.

Leonardo and Luca Pacioli's "Divine Proportion"

When Leonardo was working for Ludovico Sforza in Milan, he met and became friends with one of the most famous mathematicians of the Renaissance: Luca Pacioli. Pacioli was a Franciscan friar (a type of Catholic priest) who loved math and wrote several books about mathematics that were read and studied by people all over Europe. Pacioli traveled throughout Italy, teaching math at universities, and was invited to go to Milan to teach math in Sforza's court.

Luca Pacioli (1445–1514)

Luca Pacioli is known today as the father of modern accounting, but during the Renaissance he was the most influential mathematician of his time. Pacioli wrote two famous books. The first one was called The Collected Knowledge of Arithmetic, Geometry, Proportion and Proportionality *and was a summary of all the mathematics that the world knew at the time. It covered arithmetic, algebra,*

geometry, and trigonometry, and it was the basis for a lot of changes in mathematics that took place during the Renaissance. It also included an explanation of double-entry bookkeeping, which was the method ancient Venetian merchants used to keep track of their business accounts. This is what he's most known for today. Pacioli also wrote The Divine Proportion, *which Leonardo illustrated, and which explained many aspects of geometry and the importance of proportion.*

Both Leonardo and Luca Pacioli were interested in the connections between math and art, and they became fast friends. When Pacioli asked Leonardo if he would like to illustrate his book on geometry called *The Divine Proportion*, Leonardo agreed, and Leonardo's illustrations for Luca Pacioli's book helped influence the way people viewed geometric forms forever afterward.

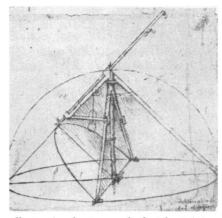

Illustration by Leonardo for The Divine Proportion.

Leonardo drew three-dimensional images of the polygons (many-sided figures) that Pacioli described in his book. These were the first illustrations Leonardo ever made for a book, and were remarkable for two major reasons.

First, Leonardo drew the polygons with "open" rather than solid faces, which meant that people could see through the front and back of the shape and get a better idea of how it was constructed. Second, no one had ever drawn polygons like these before—scholars learned about proportion and geometry through calculations and formulas, but no one had drawn them in such a way that the concepts could be seen in action.

Leonardo's illustrations were hugely helpful not only to people who studied mathematics, but also for artists and architects. In fact, the illustrations helped inspire a new trend in an art called intarsia, which is the art of making mosaics out of inlaid pieces of wood.

Leonardo and Intarsia

Leonardo's drawings of geometrical shapes inspired many intarsia artists to include his designs in their artwork. To make intarsia, an artist would use a drawing as a template for cutting many small pieces of wood (sometimes more than a thousand). The artist would then construct the intarsia by gluing the pieces of wood together in complicated patterns to create an overall scene. Intarsia was most popular during the 1520s and many of the most beautiful intarsia that are still around today have geometric forms that were based on Leonardo's drawings.

Build It Yourself

Make Your Own Open-Faced Geometric Figures

Leonardo's illustrations for Luca Pacioli's book, *The Divine Proportion*, included many complicated geometric forms called polyhedra (three-dimensional polygons). Here are the instructions for building an open-faced octahedron (8-faced figure), an icosahedron (20-faced figure), and a rhombicuboctahedron (26-faced figure).

What you'll need

- mini marshmallows or small jellybeans
- round toothpicks (you can also use square or flat toothpicks, but they are not as uniform in size and tend to snap more easily)

1.
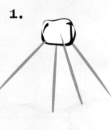

What to do

Octahedron:

1 Take a marshmallow and stick four toothpicks into it, angled out from the center of the marshmallow. This will be the top of your octahedron.

2.
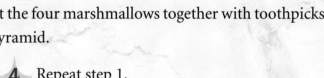

2 Attach marshmallows to the other end of each toothpick.

3 Connect the four marshmallows together with toothpicks, making a pyramid.

3.

4.
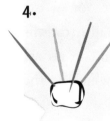

4 Repeat step 1.

5 Attach the ends of the toothpicks to the corresponding marshmallows on the bottom of your pyramid. You'll have a three-dimensional diamond shape, which is an octahedron!

5.
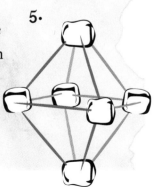

Where do the names of the polyhedra come from?

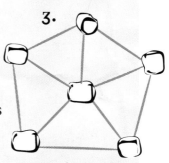

1.

Icosahedron:

1 Take one marshmallow, and attach five toothpicks so it looks like a starfish.

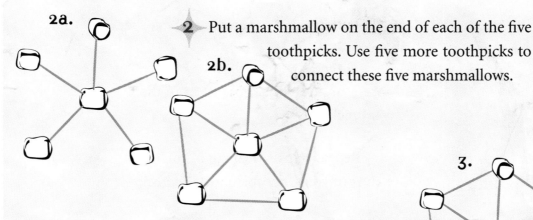

2a.

2 Put a marshmallow on the end of each of the five toothpicks. Use five more toothpicks to connect these five marshmallows.

2b.

3.

3 Repeat steps one and two. You'll now have the two halves of your icosahedron.

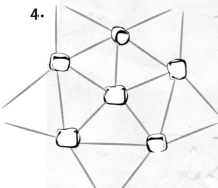

4.

4 Take one of the halves and turn it into a star by attaching two toothpicks to each marshmallow (except for the one in the middle).

5 Bend down the toothpicks you just attached and insert the points into the corresponding marshmallows on the other half of the icosahedron to complete the figure.

5.

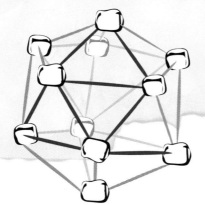

Rhombicuboctahedron:

1 Start with four marshmallows and four toothpicks. Attach them to make a square.

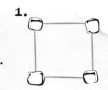

1.

2 Attach two toothpicks to the marshmallows in every corner of the square at right angles to each other.

2.

3. & 4.

3 Make four additional squares from the toothpicks.

4 Repeat steps 1 through 3. You'll have two halves of your rhombicuboctahedron.

5 Attach toothpicks to the corners of each square on both halves.

5.

6 Take one half, and stick a toothpick in the bottom of each marshmallow on the outside edge.

7 Attach these toothpicks to the outside edges of the other half. You'll have to bend down the toothpicks to make them fit. The result will look just like a soccer ball.

6.

Bend these down to line up with the corners of other half.

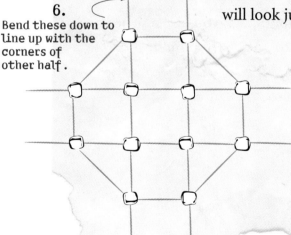

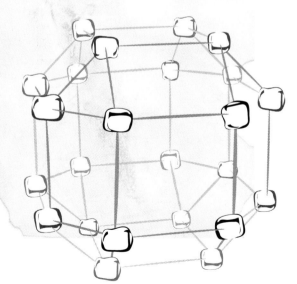

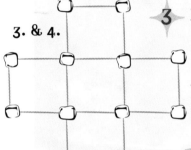

Leonardo the Jokester

While we tend to think of Leonardo as a serious artist and inventor, he was known to his friends as a joker who loved to play pranks, tell jokes and funny stories, and create rebuses and puzzles for other people to solve.

Some of Leonardo's jokes seem kind of mean or disgusting: he loved to make stinkballs out of decomposing animal and fish parts, light them, and leave the room while his friends were in there. Once he invited friends over and then filled the room with a giant sheep's intestine. Here's how it happened: Leonardo placed a sheep's intestine that was attached to a large bellows in a room, then invited his friends inside. Then he snuck out and pumped air into the intestines with the bellows. The sheep's intestine acted like a giant balloon, filling up with so much air it filled the entire room, squishing Leonardo's guests against the walls.

Another time, Leonardo brought a box into a room and told people there was a dragon inside it. When he opened the box, out came what looked like a small, very fierce dragon, which completely frightened his friends. It turns out that Leonardo had simply glued fake wings and a horn onto a lizard, but it tricked his friends and made him laugh.

Leonardo's dragon.

bellows: pumps air

37

Leonardo's "Prophecies:"

Men will walk and not move, speak with People who are not there, and hear someone who does not speak. Answer: dreams

Something else which, the closer you get to it, the more unpleasant and harmful it is. Answer: fire

Many will be those who grow as they fall. Answer: a snowball rolling on snow

Much of the sea will fly up to heaven, and for a long time will not return. Answer: how clouds are made

Leonardo also enjoyed the kinds of tricks that made him seem something of a magician. He would make multicolored flames leap out of a cup of boiling oil by throwing red wine on it, or lick the end of a stick and make it write with black ink. He made small wax animals, then filled them with warm air so they floated around the room among his guests.

Leonardo also was really interested in puzzles and liked to tell people his "prophecies." They were riddles, but rather than posing the riddle as a question, Leonardo would make a statement about something that sounded really mystical and a little creepy, but had a really simple, common answer. For example, one of Leonardo's prophecies said, "Many will have food taken out of their mouths," which sounds kind of disturbing. But the answer is, simply, "an oven."

Another kind of puzzle Leonardo loved combined drawing and words in what is called a rebus. Rebuses are puzzles in which a word or phrase has to be guessed from a picture or diagram, and Leonardo really enjoyed coming up with many different kinds of them. For example, the Italian word for "pear" is *pera*, and Leonardo drew the letter "o" and a picture of a pear to make a rebus for the word "opera."

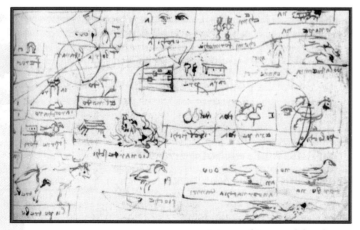

A page of Leonardo's rebuses.

Build It Yourself

Make Your Own Floating Animal

What you'll need

- pen or pencil
- cardboard or file folder (for pattern)
- wax paper
- scissors
- white glue

What to do

1 Draw template A onto the cardboard and cut out. This will be the pattern for your "gores," the panels that will make up the ball that will be the base for your floating animal.

template A

2 Using your template, trace and cut out eight wax paper gores.

3 Cut two 2-inch-diameter circles out of wax paper. These will be the ends of your balls.

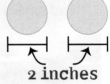

2 inches

4 Take two of the gores. Put a single strip of glue down one long side of one gore, then attach the second gore. Do this four times so that you have four double gores.

Glue together to make four double gores.

Glue down one side of one gore.

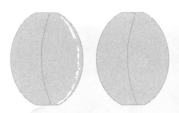

Glue together 2 double gores.

This will make half of the ball. Repeat so you have two halves with four panels each.

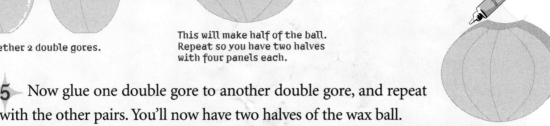

Glue together one side of each half.

5 Now glue one double gore to another double gore, and repeat with the other pairs. You'll now have two halves of the wax ball.

6 Glue one side of the half ball together, but not both sides.

7 Take one of the small circles and put glue on it. Press the ends of the gores onto it so they are completely covered. Let dry.

8 Carefully glue the last edge of the gores together.

Glue one of the circles to the top.

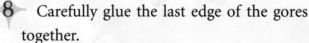

Glue last edges of gores together.

9 Now cut out a small hole (about ½-inch in diameter) in the center of the second wax-paper circle. Glue this second circle onto the other end of the ball.

10 Cut ears out of another piece of wax paper. Glue them to the sides of the ball. You can decorate your wax animal by drawing a face on it.

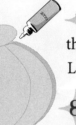

Make a hole in the second circle and glue to the bottom of the ball.

To make your wax animal float, gently blow air into the hole in the bottom of the ball. It will fill up with air, and you can bat it up so it floats. If your gores are leaking air, add a little glue to seal the seams. You can also use a hair dryer on very low airflow to fill your animal with air.

Decorate by drawing a face and gluing ears onto the ball.

Build It Yourself

Make Your Own Invisible Ink

While no one can be sure how Leonardo managed to make his stick write with black ink, it probably had something to do with what he put on the paper to begin with. Invisible "ink" is usually made from a basic substance (such as baking soda) and then "revealed" with an acidic one (such as wine or juice). For example, Leonardo may have coated a piece of paper with a basic solution (something like baking soda and water). He then could have put a little wine in his mouth, licked the stick, and then put the stick onto the coated paper. The acid from the wine would interact with the base of the baking soda, making it look like the stick magically wrote. You can make invisible ink with either juice or milk.

Juice Invisible Ink

What you'll need
- baking soda and water
- Q-tip or paintbrush
- white paper
- grape or cranberry juice
- paintbrush or sponge

What to do

1 Mix together about ¼ cup of baking soda and ¼ cup of water.

2 Dip the Q-tip or paintbrush into the mixure and write a message on a piece of clean, white paper. Let dry completely.

3 To read the secret message, paint juice across the paper.

Why does this work?

Because the juice is acidic and the baking soda is a base, and the two interact when they touch.

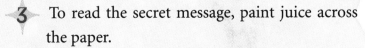

Milk Invisible Ink

What you'll need
- milk
- Q-tip or toothpick
- paper
- heat source (a light bulb works great)

What to do

1 Dip the Q-tip or toothpick into the milk and write your message on a clean piece of white paper. Let it dry completely.

2 To read it, pass it closely under a light bulb. The paper will heat up and the message will appear, written in brown.

Why does this work? Milk is acidic and slightly corrodes and weakens the paper. When the heat source is put near the paper, the weaker part begins to brown before the rest of the paper does. This works with lemon juice and any other highly acidic juice, as well.

base—a substance characterized by a bitter taste and a slippery feel that reacts with an acid to make salts

acid—a substance characterized by a sour taste that reacts with a base to form salts

Monster Shield

When Leonardo was still an apprentice in Verrocchio's studio, he practiced many different kinds of art, from metal working, to drawing, to working with clay. But painting was his true talent. One of the most famous stories about Leonardo is the story of one of his first paintings, which wasn't on canvas, but rather on a wooden shield his father asked him to decorate.

One day, Leonardo's father was given a shield by one of the tenant farmers who worked his land. The tenant farmer said he had carved the shield, and asked Leonardo's father if he would bring it to Florence and have it decorated by one of the artists there. Of course Leonardo's father brought it home for Leonardo to paint.

Leonardo reshaped and polished the shield and decided that the picture on the shield should terrify anyone who saw it. So Leonardo brought all kinds of creatures into his room— lizards, bats, grasshoppers, and locusts—turning his room into a kind of laboratory. He dissected the animals and attached parts of some of the creatures to parts of the others. The creature he made was "so horrible and fearful that it seemed to poison the air with its fiery breath." Leonardo painted onto the shield an image of this strange creature emerging from between some craggy rocks, with smoke coming out of its nostrils and fire shooting from its eyes.

When Leonado's father came to pick up the shield, Leonardo told him to wait outside his room until he was ready. Leonardo put the shield on an easel, in a small ray of light coming from the window, and darkened the rest of the room. When his father opened the door, the only thing he could see was a scary creature that looked like it was jumping out at him. Leonardo's father was frightened, and Leonardo was thrilled.

"so horrible and fearful that it seemed to poison the air with its fiery breath."

Leonardo's father liked the shield Leonardo created so much that he went out and bought a cheap wooden shield with a picture of a heart with an arrow through it to give to his tenant, and then sold the shield Leonardo had painted to a merchant in Florence for 100 ducats (gold coins), a large sum of money at the time.

Leonardo always believed that the best fantasy creatures should be based on real models: to paint a dragon, Leonardo said, take the "head of a mastiff or a pointer, the eyes of a cat, the ears of a porcupine, the muzzle of a greyhound, the brow of a lion, the crest of an old rooster, and the neck of a tortoise."

Who Was Vasari? (1511–1574)

Giorgio Vasari was born in 1511. Although he was a trained painter and skilled architect, Vasari is best known for his biographies of Italian artists.

Vasari actually coined the term "Renaissance." His most famous work was a collection of writing entitled The Lives of the Most Celebrated Painters, Sculptors, and Architects, *translated into Emglish as* The Lives of the Artists. *Vasari wrote a history of Italian art that included biographies of the great artists of Italy, including Leonardo. He said that Leonardo must have really loved his shield project, because "he suffered much in doing it, for the smell in the room of these dead animals was very bad.".*

Giorgio Vasari

Build It Yourself

Make Your Own Monster Shield

To make your own Leonardo-type monster mask, you'll need to think up some crazy combinations of animals. Choose five different animals—they could be anything from a dog to a lizard. Use your imagination; you could use the eyes of a lizard, the nose of a dog, and the ears of a horse, for example. We've given you some ideas on page 47.

What you'll need

For the shield and mask:

- pizza box
- scissors
- tin foil
- milk jugs or other empty plastic containers
- cardboard (from old cereal boxes)
- construction paper
- coat hangers
- Ping-Pong balls
- toilet paper rolls
- milk jug caps
- duct tape
- glue
- paint, feathers, leaves, glitter, or other decorations

For the papier-mâché:

- plenty of newspapers, torn or cut into 2-inch wide strips
- white paper torn into strips for the top layer so that it's easier to paint

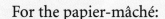

Strips of old newspaper

- flour
- water
- salt
- a big bowl

What to do

1 First, cut a large circle from the pizza box. Save the remnants—you'll need a piece to make a handle for the shield. Design your "monster" to fit onto this circle. Be creative! Make a rough sketch of your ideas before you start building and figure out the best materials for each part of your shield.

2 Gather the materials you'll need from around your house—ask your parents if it's okay to use the things that you find.

3 Begin construction, using tape and glue to fasten the materials tightly to the pizza-box shield. Allow everything to dry so that it is secure.

4 If you decide to use papier-mâché, mix one part water to one part flour. Add a couple of teaspoons of salt. The mixture should be a little thinner than white glue. Mix thoroughly so that it's smooth.

Tape on milk jug cut in half.

Tape on toilet paper rolls.

Use construction paper to cut out tongue and fangs.

Cover shield with paper-mâché.

Cut ears, tongue and fangs out of construction paper.

Ping pong balls can add fun touches.

After paper-mâché dries, you are ready to paint.

5 Dip the newspaper into the mixture, and wipe off the excess before applying the newspaper to the shield, one strip at a time. Repeat this until the entire shield and monster is covered, overlapping the newspaper pieces as you go. If you decide that you want it to be white (for easier painting), do a top layer of white paper. There should be no more than three layers of papier-mâché on the shield.

6 Allow to dry completely. This may take a couple of days, depending on the humidity in the air. If you place your shield in the sun it may dry faster, but it is more likely to crack.

Ideas for the Shield

Need some ideas? Here are a few:
- *Make horns out of toilet paper rolls.*
- *Make big, round eyes out of Ping-Pong balls.*
- *Make a snout out of a small yogurt container.*
- *Make a large face out of a half-gallon milk container.*
- *Make all different shapes on the shield surface using tinfoil.*
- *Make a big nose or mouth using a large yogurt container.*
- *Make freckles, eyes, nose, or ears out of milk jug caps.*

7 When your papier-mâché has dried, you can begin decorating. Use paint, feathers, buttons, natural objects from outside, or other items to decorate and make your monster look the way you want it to.

8 To make a handle, cut one edge of the pizza box at both corners. You'll have a long strip that has been folded over to make the side of the box. Cut the strip to a size that will fit on the back of your shield. Bend the ends of the strip down so you can tape them to the back of the shield, but still have enough room to fit your hand underneath (see diagram). Tape the edges of the handle to the pizza box with duct tape.

Cut at corners.

Side of box folded over when box is made.

Fold ends under.

Tape ends to back of shield.

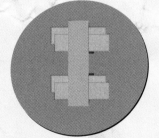

Leonardo's Useful Machines

Say your parents ask you to do some chores around the house: maybe help out with the laundry, or do the dinner dishes. Sure, it's probably not exactly what you want to do with your free time, but you throw some clothes into the washing machine or load up the dishwasher and off you go. Now picture having to do these jobs without a washing machine or dishwasher—better yet, imagine that you have to get water from a pump three blocks away, and carry it home in a bucket.

Doing everyday chores today is very different from when Leonardo was alive: 500 years ago there was no electricity, no indoor plumbing, and no cleaning products or household machines to make life easier. Everything was made by hand, and completing tasks and making products, whether they were shoes or works of art, took a great deal of time.

During the Renaissance there were no set hours for working like we have today—people didn't head off to work at nine o'clock and come home at five o'clock, five days a week, with weekends off. Instead, people's work hours were usually set by the nature of their work, by the seasons, or both. When the days became longer and the sun shone for more hours, people worked longer. During the winter months people worked less because there was less daylight.

People's work was also usually

much more closely connected with their homes. For example, if you were a baker, your home was also the site of your bakery. If you were a tailor, your shop and house were the same place. Some industries that were especially dirty, such as dyeing, tanning, and butchering, were usually grouped together in an out-of-the-way place, but most businesses were set up where people lived.

People also didn't rely on a clock to tell them when to start and finish their workday. In fact, clocks didn't even have minute hands during the Renaissance; rather, they kept time to the hour, and people usually relied on a clock in the village square to keep time for them, showing the hours, and ringing in the morning, at midday, and in the evening.

Unlike today, where people are usually paid for the amount of time they work, people in Leonardo's day were often paid a set amont for each product they made, which is called piecework. Workers would agree on a price for each item they produced, and that would be how much they received, regardless of how long they spent producing it. For example, Leonardo wrote in his notebook that he and the monks of San Donato agreed on a sum of 150 florins for him to paint *Adoration of the Magi*, no matter how long it took him. (Unfortunately for the monks, Leonardo never finished the painting at all!)

So it's really no surprise that a thinker or inventor like Leonardo spent a great deal of time observing people working around him, and coming up with ideas for machines to make their jobs easier. Some of these machines were very simple, such as an adjustable wrench that could help hold different-sized things together more securely. Some were quite intricate, such as a machine

Worth Its Weight in Gold

During the Renaissance there was no paper money, only gold, silver, and copper coins, which took their value from their mass and purity. This meant that not all silver coins would be worth the same amount, because their worth depended on their weight.

To make things even more confusing, different cities had different units and names for money: in Venice, they had ducats; in Rome, scudi; and in Florence, florins. Figuring out just how much money your money was worth was tricky business.

Did Leonardo REALLY Invent the Bicycle?

Many of Leonardo's inventive ideas were too complicated to build in his day and age because the necessary technology was lacking. Oftentimes, all he could do was dream them up and draw them. In 1967, an American man named Jules Piccus discovered some of Leonardo's most imaginative drawings in the National Library of Madrid. One of these sketches features a bicycle that looks very much like the bicycles we ride today. The bicycle was patented by Karl Drais 325 years after Leonardo drew this famous picture, which would mean that Leonardo is the true inventor! But not everyone gives Leonardo the credit for this invention. Many believe that the drawing is a fake. There is evidence that it could have been drawn in the 1960s while the monks at Grottaferrata (near Rome) were restoring the folio of drawings that contained it. But this evidence is not conclusive. Did one of the monks draw the bicycle? Did someone sneak into the Ambrosian Library where it was kept and do the deed? Or did Leonardo himself create the drawing? Unless Italian authorities allow a thorough, scientific investigation, the world may never know.

designed to make coins that were the same size and weight. Leonardo invented all sorts of machines for a variety of industries: he developed a nail-making machine so carpenters could make nails quickly and easily; designed a giant mirror to enable dyeing vats to be powered by a solar boiler; drew many different models for digging canals and dredging channels; and drew designs for drills, hydraulic-powered saws, machines that made rope, and machines for grinding grains. Like so many of Leonardo's inventions, most of these machines weren't built during his lifetime or for many centuries after that. Some, though, were used by Italians for years and some are still in use today. Leonardo developed a light using a box with a glass lens on one side and a candle inside, which was used as a streetlamp in Milan for more than 200 years, and his drawings for links of chain look identical to the kinds of chains we use for everything from bicycles to chainsaws today.

dyeing—to color permanently

The Camera Obscura

One of the scientific concepts Leonardo was most interested in was optics—how a human eye works. The common idea of the time was that the eye sent out sight rays that bounced off of objects and then came back to the eye, allowing the person to see. Leonardo realized this was wrong, because it would take too much time for a sight ray to come out of the eye, bounce off something and then come back to the eye. He used the sun to explain his idea: the sun was so far away that if a person had to send out sight rays to see it, Leonardo estimated it would take a month. (Leonardo was pretty far off on how far away the sun was. He thought it was 4,000 miles away. It's really 93 million miles away.)

Leonardo thought the eye was the most important and amazing organ in the body. He wrote, "This is the eye, the chief and leader of all others," and filled hundreds of pages in his notebooks with his ideas about how the eye worked. He dissected human eyes to learn more about them, and as a result of all his studies Leonardo developed a simple projector, bifocals, and even came up with the idea for contact lenses (although he never made them). He also worked on an idea for using a giant lens to harness solar energy for the tanning and dyeing industry, and many historians and scientists believe that he came up with the idea of a telescope long before Hans Lippershey, the Dutchman who is credited with inventing the telescope in 1608. Leonardo said, ". . . in order to observe the nature of the planets, open the roof and bring the image of a single planet onto the base of a concave mirror. The image of the planet reflected by the base will show the surface of the planet much magnified."

Camera Obscura—dark room

Leonardo figured out a way to dissect eyeballs: he boiled them in water until the whites hardened, then sliced them open.

One of the most interesting optical inventions Leonardo worked with was a camera obscura. Leonardo wasn't the first person to use one of these, but he was the first person to connect the way a camera obscura worked with the way the human eye worked—and in almost every respect, he was right! A camera obscura is nothing more than a dark box (or even a very dark room) with a very small hole in one wall that lets in light. Directly across from the hole the image from the outside world will be projected onto the wall upside down. This happens because light travels in a straight line, but when some of the rays reflected from a bright subject pass through a small hole, they become distorted (imagine trying to cram an object into a space that is too small for it) and end up as an upside-down image.

Leonardo realized that this is exactly how the human eye sees things: light reflects off the object you are viewing and passes through a small opening on the surface of the eye (your pupil), and the image gets flipped upside down. Leonardo said, "No image, even of the smallest object, enters the eye without being turned upside down." What he couldn't answer was how a human eye actually sees the image right-side up. We now know that the eye's optic nerve sends the image to the brain, which flips it right-side up. So the only thing the camera obscura lacks is a brain to flip the image!

The First Photographs

Despite its name, a camera obscura isn't a camera in the way we think of a camera—it doesn't take a photo that we can hold or put in a frame. The first photographs were taken by a French chemist named Joseph Nicephore Niepce in 1827. Niepce set up a camera obscura and put a polished pewter plate coated with a type of asphalt known as bitumen of Judea in it. After eight hours, Niepce washed the plate with a mixture of oil of lavender and white petroleum, which dissolved away the parts of the bitumen that had not been hardened by light. The result was the very first kind of photograph. Because the only way to capture an image was to let the pewter plate sit in the sun for up to eight hours, Niepce couldn't take images of people.

Build It Yourself

Make Your Own Camera Obscura

Here are directions for making two different kinds of camera obscura. One model is like a small room, and the other is portable. Both use exactly the same principal: light rays come into a dark space and reflect an inverted (upside-down) image on the opposite wall.

Camera Obscura #1

What you'll need
- potato chip or tennis ball canister with lid
- Xacto knife
- duct tape
- pushpin
- foil

Measure up 2 inches from bottom and cut

What to do

1 Start with a clean, dry canister. Cut the canister apart about 2 inches from the bottom.

2 Put the lid on the shorter piece of the can, then put the longer part of the can on top of that. Tape them together so they are secure.

Place cap on short bottom piece of can

3 If you are using a clear tennis ball canister, you will need to cover the entire can in duct tape to make the interior dark enough to see a reflected image.

Put top part of canister onto bottom piece and tape in place

4 Poke a hole in the bottom of the short end—or the end with a metal lid.

Poke a hole in the bottom of the canister

Cover canister with foil and tape in place

5 To keep as much light out of the tube as possible, wrap the entire can in foil. Tape the foil to the sides and tuck any extra into the top.

You should NEVER look directly at the sun!

6 Go outside and hold the tube with the pinhole end up to your eye. You may need to cup your hands around the eye opening of the tube to block out any extra light from the eye opening.

View through the open end

7 You should be able to see an upside down image of whatever you are viewing on the inside lid.

Camera Obscura #2

What you'll need

- 1 large box, like a refrigerator or appliance box that is large enough to get inside and literally make a "dark room"
- Xacto knife
- white sheet of paper

What to do

1 Cut a hole in the side of the box no bigger than 3 inches by 5 inches. If you are using a large packing box, make the hole smaller: around 1 inch by 3 inches.

Cut hole no bigger than 3 inches by 5 inches

2 Pull the box over you so that you are completely covered on all sides. Bring the sheet of paper with you. The only light coming into the box should come through the hole you cut.

Hold paper against this side of the box inside.

You are inside the box with the piece of paper.

What image do you think you will see on the piece of paper?

3 Hold up the piece of white paper on the side opposite the hole. You may have to move the paper a little bit to find the image, but you should be able to see an exact, upside-down replica of the image outside the box reflected on the paper.

Leonardo's Weather Predictions

Hygrometers measure the moisture in the air, and can help predict weather changes.

ARISTOTLE

Meteorology, which is the science of the earth's atmosphere and weather, was not well developed in Leonardo's day. There were no local weather forecasters who could explain that the next few days would be cloudy, or tell that the winter would be harsh or mild. Rather, people in the Renaissance looked toward the ancient Greeks, and especially the Greek philosopher Aristotle, to understand the weather and the earth's atmosphere. Aristotle first came up with the term meteorology in 340 BCE, when he wrote a book that discussed his theories about the natural world, including clouds, rain, snow, hail, lightning and thunder, and climate. Aristotle gave the book the title *Meteorologica* because in ancient Greece, anything that fell from the sky or was suspended in the sky (such as mist or fog) was called a meteor.

In *Meteorologica*, Aristotle wrote about many aspects of weather that researchers today still study, such as how lightning is caused, why different areas have different amounts of rainfall, where winds originate, and the relationship between the height of clouds and the amount of rainfall they generate. Many of Aristotle's observations about the weather were very accurate and detailed.

Sketch of hygrometer designed by Leonardo.

For example, in one section of *Meteorologica* he describes hail:

Hail is ice, and water freezes in winter; yet hailstorms occur chiefly in spring and autumn and less often in the late summer, but rarely in winter and then only when the cold is less intense. And in general hailstorms occur in warmer, and snow in colder places.

The problem with Aristotle's *Meteorologica* is that the explanations he gave for what caused the weather he observed were usually wrong. Why? Because he based all of his explanations on the assumption that the earth was the center of the universe, and that the elements of earth, water, air, and fire made up everything in the world, including weather.

Even so, for more than 2,000 years, Aristotle's ideas about weather were accepted as fact; after all, anyone could see how water moved through the earth and its atmosphere simply by watching it rain or snow. But since water vapor is invisible, no one quite understood its properties. During the Renaissance, people began to think more about the natural world and the aspects of weather that weren't visible to the naked eye. How could people predict whether it was going to rain? What caused the air to feel so heavy on hot summer days when there were no clouds in the sky? Nicholas of Cusa, a German cardinal and mathematician, in 1450 became the first person to concieve a weather instrument, when he described a hygrometer, an instrument that could measure the amount of humidity in the air. His idea was as follows:

Nicholas of Cusa

If someone should hang a good deal of wool, tied together on one end of a large pair of scales, and should balance it with stones at the other end in a place where the air is temperate it would be found that the weight of the wool would increase when the air became more humid, and decrease when the air tended to dryness.

There is no record that Nicholas of Cusa ever built his hygrometer, but Leonardo did. In 1481, he took the description and used it to create his own model.

Build It Yourself

Make Your Own Hygrometer

Here's an easy way to measure the amount of humidity in the air.

What you'll need
- two 1-pint milk or juice cartons
- scissors
- old candle
- matches
- wire coat hanger
- string
- sponge or cotton balls

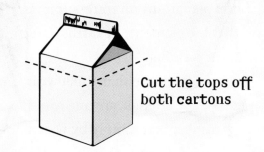

Cut the tops off both cartons

What to do

1 Cut the tops off the milk cartons so you have two equal-sized containers.

2 Melt a thin coating of wax on the bottom of one container.

Coat the bottom of one carton with wax

Poke a hole in each side

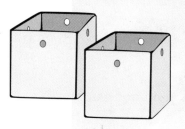

3 Poke holes in each side of the containers and thread string through them.

4 Tie the string ends to the ends of the coat hanger, so one container is at each end.

5 Put some cotton balls or a sponge in the container without the wax coating.

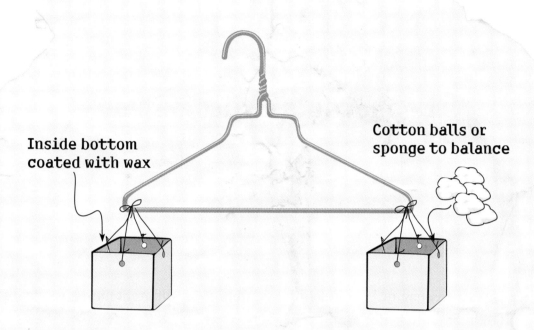

Inside bottom coated with wax

Cotton balls or sponge to balance

6 Hang the hanger outside where it won't be affected by wind, then add more cotton or pieces of sponge to the second container so that the two containers are level and balanced.

7 Leave your hygrometer outside, checking it every ten minutes to see if the container with the cotton or sponge has grown heavier than the container with the wax. If the container with the sponge or cotton balls has grown heavier, it means the humidity level of the air is rising—the higher the humidity, the more water vapor in the atmosphere.

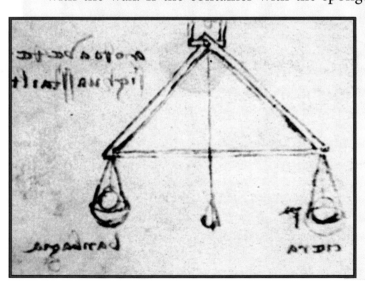

Leonardo's hygrometer.

Leonardo's Hydrometer

It is easy to imagine Leonardo thinking about why different liquids weigh different amounts—for example why a cup of water weighs less than the same amount of honey—and trying to figure out a way to measure the difference. After all, it's easy to understand why a five-inch square of concrete is more dense than a five-inch square of wood—you can hold the two blocks in your hands and feel the difference. But how could people determine how dense one liquid was in relation to another? Leonardo came up with an idea for an invention that would help measure this. Called a hydrometer, his device measured the densities of different liquids, based on a principal explained by the ancient Greek scientist Archimedes. Archimedes said that a solid suspended in a liquid will be buoyed up by a force equal to the weight of the liquid displaced. That means that the lower the density of the liquid, the lower the hydrometer will sink.

Density vs. Viscosity

What's the difference between density and viscosity? Density measures how much mass a liquid (or anything else) has—how much the liquid weighs. Viscosity measures the liquid's thickness. If you compare a cup of honey and a cup of water, you'll find that honey has greater density than water (a cup of honey will weigh slightly more than a cup of water). Honey is also more viscous: stick a spoon into the cup of honey and a spoon into the cup of water and then try to pull them out quickly. You'll find it's much harder to pull the spoon out of the honey.

Build It Yourself

Make Your Own Hydrometer

You can build your own hydrometer to measure the density of different liquids.

What you'll need
- ruler with centimeter marks
- fine-tip permanent marker
- a straight straw
- three glasses, water, salt, dishwashing liquid
- a small piece of clay
- two small nails that slip inside the straw

What to do

1 Create a scale on your straw, so you'll be able to easily judge where it floats in liquid. Mark half centimeter marks with your permanent marker on the straw, from the top to about three-quarters of the way down.

2 Plug the bottom of the straw with the clay so that no water leaks into the straw.

3 Drop the two small nails into the straw, one on top of the other, so they sit at the bottom against the clay.

Drop nails into straw

Plug bottom of straw with clay material

Do you float better in fresh or salt water? Why? What does this tell you about the composition of the water?

4 Take three glass containers, preferably with narrow mouths. Fill one up with normal tap water. Fill another up with warm tap water, add a handful of salt to the water, and let it dissolve. (Salt will dissolve more quickly in warm water.) Fill the third with tap water and add dish detergent. Carefully mix the detergent with the water.

5 Gently place your hydrometer in each glass, noting where the mark on the hydrometer is in relation to the top of the glass. Which liquid is the most dense? Which liquid is the least dense? How can you tell?

Hydrometer in Action: Maple Syrup Making

When you pour maple syrup on your waffles or pancakes you may not know that a hydrometer helped make the syrup taste great. Maple syrup comes from boiled maple sap, a liquid that sugarmakers collect from maple trees in the early spring. Maple sap is mostly water; in fact, to make just one gallon of maple syrup, sugarmakers have to boil 40 gallons of maple sap. The excess water boils off, while the sugars of the sap remain. Since so much liquid is boiling, sugarmakers rely on both a hydrometer and a thermometer to know when the sap has boiled long enough to turn to syrup. When the temperature of the liquid is 219 degrees Fahrenheit (7 degrees higher than the temperature of boiling water) and the sugar-to-water ratio measured by the hydrometer is 66 percent, the syrup is ready.

Leonardo's Monkey Wrench

Most history books will tell you that the monkey wrench, a type of adjustable wrench that can fit many different kinds of bolts, was invented in 1858 by a man named Charles Moncky, who developed it for use repairing locomotives. But what those history books don't mention is that almost 400 years earlier, Leonardo drew a design for a wrench that looked amazingly like the early wrenches Moncky and other railroad workers used on their locomotives. In Leonardo's design, an adjustable bolt holds the jaw piece to the larger handle, which creates a J-shaped wrench. The adjustable bolt allows the jaw to move closer to or farther from the handle, so it adjusts to different-sized objects.

In Leonardo's time, nuts and bolts were just coming into popular use; the first wrenches were not adjustable, making it tough to fix anything with efficiency. The monkey wrench made it possible to tighten or loosen many different-sized nuts and bolts with the same tool. In his ongoing quest to come up with new ways to make regular jobs easier and more efficient, Leonardo also invented or drew sketches of large pliers for heavier work (which worked the same way as the monkey wrench, with an adjustable jaw) and a clamp-and-screw type of device to remove nails. All of these became prototypes of modern tools that people use every day.

Build It Yourself

Make Your Own Monkey Wrench

This wrench uses an old garden hose instead of a metal or wood frame.

What you'll need
- 2-foot-long piece of garden hose
- pen
- hammer and large nail
- 3-inch bolt with a wing nut
- dowel rod or stick

What to do

1 Measure 10 inches down the hose, and bend it at that point into a J shape. Mark a line approximately three inches from the end of the short side of the hose across both sides of the hose.

2 Using the hammer and large nail, punch a hole through both sides of the hose where you marked the line. Work the nail around in the hole to widen it enough to fit the bolt.

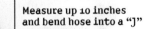

Measure up 10 inches and bend hose into a "J"

Measure up 3 inches and mark across both parts of the hose

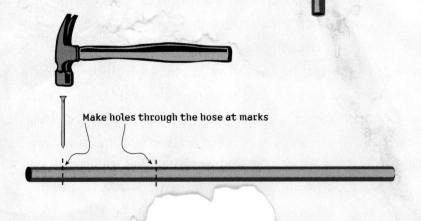

Make holes through the hose at marks

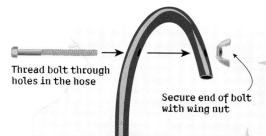

Thread bolt through holes in the hose

Secure end of bolt with wing nut

3 Push the bolt through both sides of the hose. Loosely spin the wing nut on to keep the bolt in place.

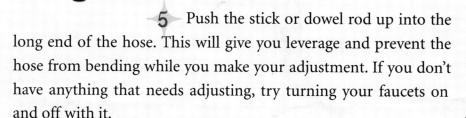

4 Put the object you want to adjust in between the curve of the hose and the bolt. Tighten the wing nut until the hose is snug against the object.

5 Push the stick or dowel rod up into the long end of the hose. This will give you leverage and prevent the hose from bending while you make your adjustment. If you don't have anything that needs adjusting, try turning your faucets on and off with it.

Insert dowel into hose as a handle

What Is a Moncky, or Monkey, Wrench, Anyway?

A monkey wrench is an adjustable wrench that can be used when a conventional wrench won't fit a bolt needing adjustment. In the days before vise grips and pocket tools, monkey wrenches were often the only tool that would work in certain situations. The monkey wrench had some problems too, which is why it isn't used very often today. It didn't work very well for precision adjustments. It also slipped around a lot, so it could be difficult and frustrating to use. Because it was liable to slip, it could even be dangerous to use, possibly flying off a bolt when a lot of force was applied to it. The combination of a flying wrench and slipping bolts made for some serious injuries. Today, we have more precise wrenches as well as adjustable wrenches such as vise grips, which have a locking arm. They are much safer, but lack the great name of the monkey wrench.

Leonardo and Water

Leonardo was fascinated by water, which he called the "vehicle of nature." He compared water's role on the earth to blood's role in the body, and believed water circulated according to fixed rules inside and outside the earth: coming from springs in the ground, running in rivers down to the sea, and falling from the sky as rain and snow.

Leonardo was also afraid of water—he had seen the Arno River in Florence burst its banks and flood the countryside twice, and he thought a lot about the destructive power of water when it was out of control. His notebooks are filled with drawings of water rising, swirling, and churning, and he drew many pictures of great floods that would wipe out everything in their path. He also spent a lot of time observing how water moved around rocks and other obstacles, how running water moved when it hit still water, and how waves formed. His drawings of water were so beautiful and accurate, in fact, that they were used by scientists for hundreds of years as diagrams for the study of water and its movement.

Archimedes water screw.

lock—a section of a canal that can be closed to control the water level

Water was the most powerful force on the planet in Leonardo's day (remember that there was no electricity at that time), and one of the least understood. Leonardo filled many notebooks with ideas for ways to harness water's incredible power, and drew hundreds of diagrams for machines that could use water power to make work easier or more efficient. Leonardo designed many machines to move water from one place to another as well as many different kinds of boats, bridges, and dams. He designed locks and canal systems—and machines for excavating canals—to connect Florence to the sea. For the city of Milan he designed a series of locks and paddle wheels to wash its dirty streets. He also looked at water with a military eye, and designed many water-based methods for attacking an enemy. He designed a hook that would attach to the side of a boat and pull the hull apart, (he also designed a double-hulled boat, probably to resist his boat hook!), a diving suit and snorkel to enable soldiers to sneak up on enemies underwater, and even a life preserver.

Leonardo also viewed water from a scientific perspective. He was one of the first people to recognize that water causes erosion. He wrote, "Water gnaws at mountains and fills valleys. If it could, it would reduce the earth to a perfect sphere." Even more amazing, Leonardo went against the popular idea that fossils of shells found in the mountains came either from the biblical flood or had somehow grown in the rocks. Instead, he decided that based on common sense and science—and his own study of water—the only way shells could be found in the layers of rock in the mountains was for them to have been buried at a time before the mountains existed.

Life preserver.

Leonardo's dredging machine.

After all, Leonardo reasoned, they couldn't have been thrown up on a mountain during a flood, since falling rain would have pushed the shells downward, not upward, and receding floodwaters would have pulled the shells back down the mountain. Also, said Leonardo, the fossils in the mountains included things like oysters and coral, and it would have been impossible for one flood to carry them 300 miles inland to the Italian mountains—or for coral or oysters to crawl 300 miles in the 40 days and 40 nights of the Biblical flood. He said, "It must be presumed that in those places there were sea coasts, where all the shells were thrown up, broken, and divided . . ."

Leonardo believed that those fossils helped tell the story of the earth itself, which was far older than any human could record. He wrote, "Since things are much more ancient than letters, it is no marvel if, in our day, no records exist of these seas having covered so many countries . . . sufficient for us is the testimony of things created in the salt waters, and found again in high mountains far from the seas."

A bird's-eye view of the Arno River valley as conceived by Leonardo.

Walk-on-Water Shoes

Some of the most intriguing images Leonardo drew in his notebooks were inventions for use in the water. Many of these ideas are connected to Leonardo's war machines—he sketched a diving snorkel, an inflatable life preserver, a diving suit, and even webbed gloves, all apparently designed for soldiers to wear underwater while they sabotaged enemy ships. No one knows for sure if these were ever made, though, because Leonardo wrote in one of his notebooks that he wasn't going to show how to make them because he didn't want the instructions falling into the hands of enemies. Leonardo thought of every possible form of water transportation, including by foot: one of his drawings showed a man walking on top of the water using what looked like snowshoes and holding poles.

It is necessary to have a coat made of leather . . . quite air-tight. And when you are obliged to jump into the sea . . . let yourself be carried by the waves. . . always keep in your mouth the end of the tube through which air passes into the garment; and if . . . it should become necessary for you to take a breath when the foam prevents you, draw it through the mouth of the tube from the air within the coat.

Build It Yourself

Make Your Own Walk-on-Water Shoes

This project makes a type of walk-on-water shoe that is easy to build and lots of fun to try out. Make sure you have a parent or another adult with you when you are testing your shoes, since even Leonardo can't guarantee that you won't get wet!

What you'll need

- piece of Styrofoam "blueboard" insulation, 3 inches thick by 2 feet by 8 feet, available at any lumberyard or large hardware store*
- yardstick
- large serrated kitchen knife or small handsaw
- pen
- duct tape and scissors
- two sticks long enough to use as poles, or broom handles, old ski poles, dowel rods, etc.

*If you weigh more than 100 pounds, you will need two pieces of blueboard taped together to make a double, more buoyant set of shoes. Follow steps 1–4 twice, then securely tape the two pieces one on top of the other so that your shoes are double-layered.

What to do

1 Measure yourself against the blueboard and cut the board so one piece is the same height you are.

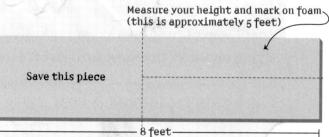

2 Cut that piece of the board in half lengthwise. You'll have two 12-inch-wide pieces.

3 Find the middle point of one end of each piece of blueboard. Measure 8 inches at an angle on both sides and cut that part off so your board looks like a ski.

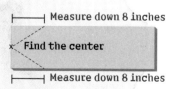

4 Do this to both pieces. These pointed ends will be the fronts of your walk-on-water shoes.

In order to make the shoes grab at the water and go forward while you're walking on them, you'll need to make some water pockets. The idea is that while you're moving forward, the pockets stay flat under the water, but when you move one foot backward, they fill with water and provide enough friction to keep up your momentum.

5 Cut six pieces of duct tape to the following lengths: 4, 5, 6, 7, 8, and 9 inches. With the sticky sides up, lay the bottom edge of the 4-inch piece on top of the 5-inch piece, then the bottom edge of the 5-inch piece on top of the 6-inch piece, and so on (see diagram). The sticky sides should all be facing up. Now cut five more pieces of duct tape to the following lengths: 3, 4, 5, 6, and 7 inches. Lay the 3-inch piece sticky-side down in the center of the five-inch piece of the other strip, the 4-inch piece sticky-side down in the center of the 6-inch piece of the other strip, and so on, until all the pieces are used up (see diagram). It should look something like a pyramid, with sticky surfaces on the top and sides. This will be one of your water pockets.

4 inches
5 inches
6 inches
7 inches
8 inches
9 inches

4-inch piece of tape

Shorter pieces of tape stuck onto longer pieces—sticky side to sticky side

6 To attach the water pocket to the bottom of one of your water shoes, first attach the top of your duct tape pyramid, then attach one side, then the other, leaving room for the pocket to expand when in the water.

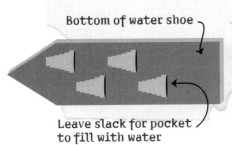

Bottom of water shoe

Leave slack for pocket to fill with water

7 Make four tape pockets for each water shoe, placing them in an alternating pattern from about 5 inches from the top of the water shoe to a little over halfway down the shoe.

Find the center of the
water shoe from front to back

4 inches

4 inches

Mark 4 inches in from inner edge.
This is approximately where
your foot holder should be attached

8 Now make your foot holders. Flip over the water shoes, and make a mark halfway down the length of the shoe. At this mark, measure 4 inches from the inside of each water shoe—this is where the top of your foot holder will go.

9 Your foot holders will be a lot like the water pockets you made, but slightly longer so your feet can fit into them easily. Cut eightpieces of duct tape in lengths of 4, 5, 6, 7, 8, 9, 10, and 11 inches, and attach them to each other using the instructions in step 5. Cut seven more pieces in lengths of 3, 4, 5, 6, 7, 8, and 9 inches, and attach them in the same way as in step 5. Attach the top of the foot holder to the board at the mark you made, then press down one side of the tape, then the other. You should have a slightly longer, slightly narrower version of the water pockets (it should look a lot like a slipper). It's a good idea to reinforce your foot holders with longer pieces of duct tape on the sides—shoving your foot into the foot holders can make them lift off the board, and if the duct tape gets wet it can come off and lose its stickiness.

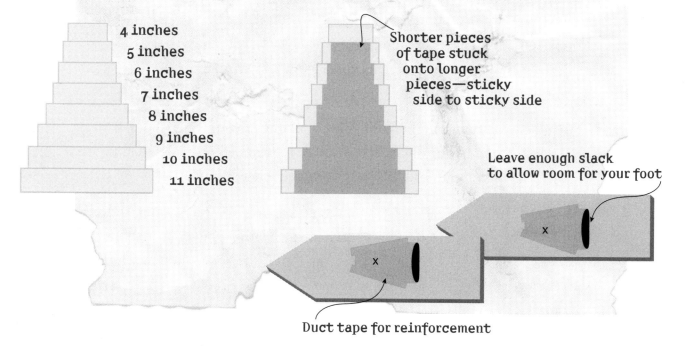

4 inches

5 inches

6 inches

7 inches

8 inches

9 inches

10 inches

11 inches

Shorter pieces
of tape stuck
onto longer
pieces—sticky
side to sticky side

Leave enough slack
to allow room for your foot

x

x

Duct tape for reinforcement

6 inches

10 Now you're ready to make your poles. Using the leftover blueboard measure two 6-inch-by-6-inch squares and cut them out. If you want, you can cut the corners off of the squares to make them more rounded. Jab the sticks into the centers of the squares—these are your poles for walking on water, and will help with balance.

11 Now get on the water and try to walk!

Leonardo's Invention Used Today

So do you think anyone ever used this crazy idea of Leonardo's? One wouldn't think so—the walk-on-water shoes are fun to play around with, but most likely you wouldn't use them for general transportation.

One man did, though. Remy Bricka, a Frenchman, walked 3,502 miles across the Atlantic Ocean in 1998. He left the Canary Islands on April 2, wearing a pair of 14-foot pontoons shaped like very large skis and carrying poles with paddles to help propel him along the surface of the water. He used motions similar to a cross-country skier to travel over the water.

Behind him, he pulled a coffin-shaped "bed" so that he could sleep, as well as a water filter so he could drink straight from the ocean. He also brought a net for catching fish as well as a GPS system so that he knew generally where he was. He did not, however, bring any extra food, and during the trek, he lost about 50 pounds, going from 160 pounds 110 pounds. Bricka walked an average of 50 miles per day, arriving in Trinidad on May 31, 1998, finishing his trek across the ocean in less than two months.

Bricka also holds the world record of fastest water-walker. He walked 1 kilometer in 7 minutes, 7.41 seconds in the Olympic pool in Montreal.

Leonardo loved **animals**, and it is said that he would **walk** through the markets in Florence and buy **caged** birds so he could let them go free.

Leonardo's Webbed Gloves

Historians have found lots of evidence that Leonardo's drawings for water inventions aren't entirely new. In fact, many of his ideas have been found in documents from ancient times—webbed gloves, for example, have been mentioned in documents dating back to the ancient Greeks. And other Renaissance artists and thinkers were also working on ideas for inventions that would allow people to tame water. The Renaissance artist and architect, Leon Battista Alberti (the man who invented the theory of perspective), for example, designed diving equipment for the purpose of recovering some ancient Roman ships that had sunk to the bottom of an Italian lake.

Leonardo sketched his idea for a pair of gloves that would work like fins some time between 1487 and 1490; when he sketched the gloves, it appears he was mainly thinking about how someone could use them to survive in a storm or tempest. The annotation under the drawing says "*guanto con pannicoli per nuotare in mare,*" which means "glove with membranes for swimming in the sea," and the glove appears to be part of an outfit to help people float, especially in emergency situations. Leonardo's gloves were designed to be tied around the wrists and would likely have been made of leather with wooden ribs to stiffen them. They were shaped kind of like a seabird's foot. Leonardo's gloves probably weren't ever made or used during his time, but if you look around today, webbed gloves are everywhere. Water fitness classes, scuba divers, and even body surfers use webbed swim gloves to help strengthen their arms and move more efficiently when they swim.

"*guanto con pannicoli per nuotare in mare*"

Build It Yourself

Make Your Own Webbed Gloves

What you'll need

- rubber cleaning gloves, latex gloves, old leather gloves, or any non-cloth gloves that you don't mind covering in duct tape and getting soaked
- five sticks or chopsticks
- duct tape
- scissors
- permanent marker

What to do

1 This project works best with a partner. One of you will put on the gloves while the other person helps tape them together. When one pair of gloves are done, you can switch.

Palm of right hand

2 Put on a glove, and have your partner tape a chopstick to the end of each finger. The end of the chopstick should cover your last knuckle on each finger and thumb.

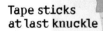

Tape sticks at last knuckle

3 Spread out your fingers so that the glove and chopsticks are splayed apart.

4 Have your partner tape the sticks attached to your middle, ring, and pinky fingers together with strips of duct tape on both sides so that it looks a little like a fan. Cover the whole chopstick.

5 Tape the sticks attached to your thumb and first finger together in the same way. You'll have a gap between your first and middle finger.

75

6 Tape the two sections together on both sides. Your hand should look like the diagram at right.

7 Cut valleys in the tape between the chopsticks so your glove looks like a webbed foot. This will help the glove move through the water more efficiently. If you goof up or don't like the way it looks, just cover it with more duct tape and start again!

8 Finally, cover the back of the glove with duct tape but don't cover the palm. Duct tape isn't stretchy, and you'll want to be able to get the glove on and off.

9 Now get in the water and start swimming!

Back of right hand

Goose

Turtle

Frog

Can you think of other creatures with webbed feet?

Nature: Invention's Great Inspiration

If you look at Leonardo's webbed gloves, you'll probably notice that they look a lot like the webbed feet of water creatures. Leonardo often looked to the natural world for invention inspiration—the most famous examples are his flying machines, which mimic the flapping of birds' wings. Other modern inventors also have used the natural world as inspiration for some pretty amazing inventions that we use everyday. One of these is Velcro. It was invented by a Swiss biologist named Georg de Mestral in 1948. Dr. Mestral was walking through a field one day when he got some cockleburs stuck to his socks. He picked them off, looked at them under a microscope, and realized that they were made up of dozens of tiny hooks that attached themselves to the fibers in his socks. Dr. Mestral designed his own kind of hooked material, and Velcro was born.

Leonardo in Flight

It's probably hard to imagine a world where you couldn't hop on an airplane to travel where you need to go, but the airplane is a relatively new invention. The first successful power-driven airplane was launched a little over 100 years ago by brothers Wilbur and Orville Wright. Their plane, *Flyer*, flew 120 feet and stayed in the air for only about 12 seconds after it took off from the sand dunes of Kitty Hawk, North Carolina.

So it's all the more amazing that more than 400 years before the Wright brothers dazzled the world with their airplane, Leonardo da Vinci was drawing and dreaming about machines that could make people fly.

Leonardo was fascinated by the idea of flying and gliding, and spent years drawing designs for gliders, flying machines, and flapping wings. He was the first person to study flight in a scientific manner: he spent hours and hours watching

From Leonardo's Notebooks

"See how the wings striking against the air hold up the heavy eagle in the thin upper air, near to the element of fire. And likewise see how the air moving over the sea strikes against the bellying sails, making the loaded heavy ship run; so that by these demonstrative and definite reasons you may know that man with his great contrived wings, battling the resistant air and conquering it, can subject it and rise above it."

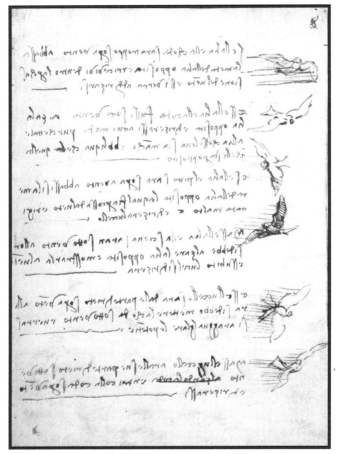

Studies of birds in flight.

birds in the air, sketching the way they dove and swooped, studying the angles of their wings at different points in flight, and observing how they turned and rode air currents to keep aloft. He also dissected birds and bats and studied their anatomy, focusing on the structure of their wings. Many of his sketches mimic the construction of a bat or bird's wing spread in flight.

Leonardo also sketched the way other things moved in air: he drew falling leaves and a glider underneath them, with a note that said, "Make tomorrow, out of various shapes of cardboard, figures descending through the air, falling from our jetty; and then draw the figures and the movements made by the descent of each, in various parts of its descent."

There is no record that any of Leonardo's flying machines worked, and in fact, most of them couldn't have been successful: they were designed to mimic the flapping of birds' wings, which would have required more strength than any human could manage. However, many of his flying machine sketches show devices that are now common on most airplanes, including moveable wing flaps to change altitude or speed, as well as landing gear.

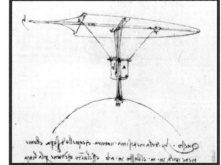

Plans for a glider.

Leonardo's Ornithopter

Leonardo's ornithopter.

Of all Leonardo's interests, none fascinated him as much as flight. He spent more than 25 years dreaming of, drawing, and building models of wings in an attempt to learn to fly. Leonardo thought birds are able to fly because they flap their wings downward and backward. In reality birds fly because the wing feathers provide thrust when the wing beats down, and the inner wing provides lift (on airplanes the engines provide thrust and the shape of the wing provides lift). In the middle years of his life, Leonardo worked on many ideas for a machine that could fly by flapping its wings. Some of Leonardo's designs tested how much weight a flapping wing could lift so that he could use the information to build an ornithopter with the correct-sized wings to carry a man off the ground. Other designs were for flying machines in which a man could stand upright, and another where he would lie down and steer with his feet. Along with drawing flapping-winged ornithopters, Leonardo also began sketching gliders with maneuverable wings. Interestingly, Leonardo actually had the theory of gliding absolutely right, and if he'd spent more time focusing on creating a working glider, some historians think he may actually have been able to fly.

Did He Really Fly?

A line in one of Leonardo's notebooks has led some historians to think that maybe Leonardo did try out at least one of his flying machines. Leonardo wrote, "The great bird will take its first flight from Mount Ceceri which will fill the universe with amazement." The story goes that one of Leonardo's students experimented with one of his flying machines by launching it off a mountain close to Leonardo's home—crashing and breaking his leg in the process—but nobody knows for sure.

Build It YourselF

Build Your Own Ornithopter

This is an interpretation of Leonardo's ornithopter. In his drawing, a person would slide into the tube and control the movements of the wings with his feet.

What you'll need
- two 20-ounce (or larger) cereal boxes
- scissors
- pencil
- paper towel tube
- scotch tape
- two rubber bands
- toothpicks (round are more durable, but flat work, too)
- piece of balsa chopstick, the lighter the better
- ruler or tape measure

Cut along line

Crunchy Flakes

What to do

1 Make sure the cereal boxes are open at both ends, then cut along one seam of each cereal box so that the box lies flat. You will have two full panels to work with.

2 Draw your first wing on one half of a cereal box. Use template A for an idea of the shape. Cut out the first wing, then use it to trace around for your second wing, so they are both the same

3 Draw and cut out template B (the tail) on the second cereal box. This will be your ornithopter's tail.

template A

template B

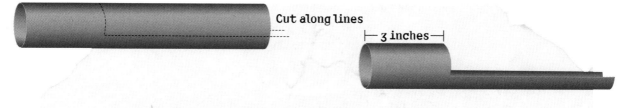

Cut along lines

⊢ 3 inches ⊣

Cut angles at end

4 Take the paper towel tube and cut up the tube on both sides, leaving about 3 inches of the tube whole. Cut off the length of tube you've slit open. This is your glider's chassis. You'll tape the tail piece onto the top of the cut end of the tube, and the wings underneath the whole end of the tube.

Tape tail onto top of chassis

5 Trim the edges of the cut end of the tube at a very slight angle so that the tail piece fits snugly. You'll have to slightly flatten the sides of the tube to fit the tail piece. Tape securely.

Tape wings onto bottom of chassis

2 inches   2 inches

2 inches   2 inches

6 Tape the wings together, then tape it to the underside of the tube.

7 Mark a point on each wing approximately 2 inches from the edge of the wing and 2 inches from where the wings attach to the chassis. Poke a hole just big enough to fit a rubber band.

8 Thread a rubber band through each hole, and on the bottom side, slide a toothpick under the rubber band so it won't slide out of the hole when pulled. Pull the rubber band tight.

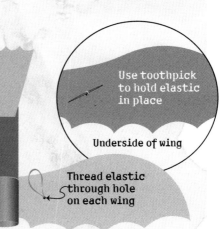

Use toothpick to hold elastic in place

Underside of wing

Thread elastic through hole on each wing

9 Poke a hole in the center of the tube just big enough to fit a piece of chopstick (or a bundle of toothpicks taped together). The chopstick should be just tall enough to stick out of the top of the tube about one-half inch.

Pull the elastics around the chopstick to create tension on the wings and raise them slightly

10 Loop the rubber bands around the chopstick until the wings come up a bit and there is enough tension on the wings to keep them flexed.

11 Hold the ornithopter right behind the wings and let her fly. You may have to adjust the rubber bands and chopstick slightly to get the maximum amount of glide.

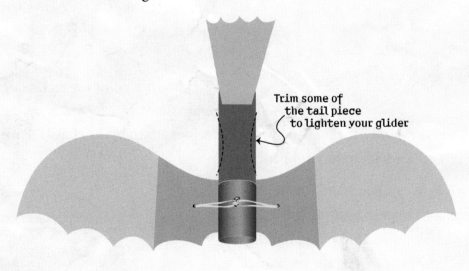

Trim some of the tail piece to lighten your glider

Hint: if you find the back half of the tube is weighing down your glider, you can trim the middle of the chassis just slightly so that it has an hourglass shape. Be careful not to cut at too great an angle or it will bend in half.

Leonardo's Helicopter

In addition to drawing several different kinds of fixed-wing gliders and flying machines with bird wings, Leonardo also began thinking about the possibilities of flying with a wing that lifted up off the ground like a screw, rather than like a bird. Around 1480, he began experimenting with the idea of using spin to lift a vehicle off the ground, and in 1482, he drew a diagram of a machine that looks a lot like a helicopter.

Just like many other Leonardo inventions, the idea for a helicopter-type machine wasn't his alone: hand-held flying toys developed by the Chinese that used the same principle of spinning lift had been around for centuries. But what Leonardo did was look at the concept of spinning lift and try to apply it to human flight. He drew a model for a helicopter-type machine that he thought could take off from the ground and called it the Helical Air Screw. In his notebook he wrote, "I have discovered that a screw-shaped device such as this, if it is well made from starched linen, will rise in the air if turned quickly."

Leonardo used his knowledge of bird anatomy to design the Helical Air Screw: his plans called for the structure to be made of hollow reeds, so it would be lightweight but also rigid and strong, and covered in starched linen, which would make the wing quite stiff but as light as possible. To power the helical screw, Leonardo called for four men to run around the central shaft, hold-

Helical Air Screw design.

ing on to a bar sticking out of the shaft. His theory was that their combined energy would make the spiral turn and create enough force to make the helicopter bore through the air like a corkscrew.

The problem is that Leonardo's design just wouldn't work: the forward action of the men pushing the shaft wouldn't provide enough power to overcome the turning effect, or torque, produced by pushing the helical screw around the central pole. Rather, the machine would stay on the ground—and eventually fling the men away. You've probably experienced this if you've ever pushed a playground whirligig as hard as you could and then tried to jump on. The force of the turning axle pushes you away, and you have to fight that force to get on.

In fact, it took more than 400 years and many other failed experiments before helicopter innovators designed a machine that could overcome the torque of a spinning axle and make a successful flight. The invention of the internal combustion engine in 1876 made it possible for inventors to get enough power to lift a rotary wing aircraft off the ground. In 1907, Frenchman Louis Bréguet built an X-shaped helicopter with four rotors (one on each end of the X) named *Gyroplane #1*, that he managed to "fly" a few inches off the ground. The age of the helicopter was born.

Leonardo the Innovator

One reason Leonardo was so successful as an inventor was that he could imagine ways to use and improve ideas and machines that already existed. For example, Leonardo designed a trumpet with keys. The trumpet (probably what we would call a bugle today) had been in existence as a military instrument for many years, but because it consisted of a plain tube, it couldn't play every note of the scale. Leonardo designed a trumpet that had keys and a second tube so that the trumpeter could play all of the notes in a scale, and actually shift musical keys. Another invention Leonardo modified was the roasting spit. Roasting spits had been around since the Egyptians, but required someone to turn the spit so the meat wouldn't burn over the fire. Leonardo designed a roasting spit that turned itself: the hot air that rose from the fire would turn a fan set into the chimney of the spit, and a shaft connected to the fan turned a set of gears that were attached to the spit—so it turned itself!

Build It Yourself

Make Leonardo's Helical Air Screw Model

This project requires the use of a drill and a hammer and nails. Make sure you have parental supervision using them, or have your parents help you.

What you'll need

- cereal box
- scissors
- mechanical compass
- pencil
- wooden dowel rod or a smooth, rounded chopstick, about 10–12 inches long and approximately ⅜ inch in diameter
- masking tape
- two small pieces of heavy-duty cardboard
- duct tape
- hammer and nail
- three small pieces of wood, approximately 6–12 inches long for use as a launcher—1-inch-by-1-inch vegetable or garden stakes would be ideal, but any piece of wood at least 1 inch thick is fine
- electric drill with a bit that is slightly larger than the diameter of your dowel
- string

Cut along line

Crunchy Flakes

What to do

1 Open both ends of the cereal box and cut one seam so that the cardboard lies flat.

7½ inches

2 Using a compass, draw two circles approximately 7½ inches in diameter (3¾-inch radius) on the cereal box. Cut these out.

85

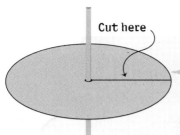

Cut here

3 Poke a hole in the center of one of the circles and push the dowel rod through it. This is the start of the air screw's wing. Cut the circle halfway through on one side.

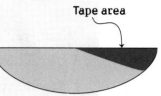

Tape area

4 Now cut the other circle in half. Tape one half of the circle to one of the cut ends of the circle on the dowel so that it is underneath the full circle.

5 Bend the upper rotor (the upper cut part of the circle) up a bit. If it starts to sag, make a tape support from the top of the dowel rod to the outer edge.

Tape support

6 Spin the air screw around a couple of times to feel if one side is heavier than the other. You may need to put a piece of tape (adding weight) on the upper rotor to balance out the tape and extra weight of the added half circle on the bottom.

7 Your helical air screw needs a base to act as a flywheel and to store the energy the twirling string will give it. Cut out two circles approximately 2 inches in diameter from the heavy-duty cardboard. Lay one on top of the other and cover the whole thing with a layer of duct tape. This will give the base a bit of weight and better rigidity.

8 With a hammer and nail make a hole in the center of the circle that will fit the dowel—make sure the dowel fits snugly in the circle. Slide the circle onto the dowel, leaving about 3 inches of the dowel below the circle.

2-inch disks
duct-taped together

flywheel—a heavy, rotating wheel used to store kinetic energy and minimize variations in the speed of spin

Nail pieces of wood together

9 Take the three pieces of wood, placing them one on top of the other. Slide the middle piece of wood back so **At least 2 inches** that there is a gap at least 2 inches long. Hammer the three pieces of wood together so you now have a single piece of wood that looks like the above diagram. You could glue the pieces of wood together with wood glue, but they will be sturdier if you nail them.

Now drill a hole through the top half and a little way into the bottom half of the piece of wood. The hole needs to be wide enough that the air screw dowel moves freely in it, but not so wide that it can't stay upright.

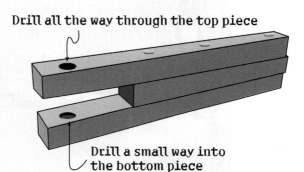

Drill all the way through the top piece

Drill a small way into the bottom piece

10 Now put the helical air screw through the holes in the launcher. Move the base so it is resting on the top part of the launcher. Wind the string in between the top and bottom parts of the launcher, hold on to the launcher, pull the string, and let her rip!

Base

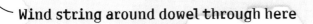

Wind string around dowel through here

Leonardo's Parachute

One of Leonardo's most famous quick sketches is of a tiny stick figure suspended from a parachute. Although he sketched it more than five centuries ago and probably never had an opportunity to try out his design, Leonardo's parachute bears an uncanny resemblance to parachutes that are used today.

Leonardo described his parachute as follows: "If a man is provided with a length of gummed linen cloth with a length of 12 yards on each side and 12 yards high, he can jump from any great height whatsoever without injury." Leonardo never got to try out his parachute from great heights (it is said that he may have tested it, but it could have only been from trees or tall buildings), but in the year 2000, hundreds of years after Leonardo first sketched his ideas, a world-renowned sky diver named Adrian Nicholas tested a model of Leonardo's parachute.

Nicholas worked for months on a replica of Leonardo's parachute. He even used canvas and wood—materials Leonardo would have had access to—and tools similar to those that Leonardo may have used. Nicholas's parachute weighed more than 187 pounds (compare that to the average modern parachute that weighs between 25 and 30 pounds). Most people who heard about Nicholas's plan were convinced the parachute wouldn't work because it was just too heavy. One safety measure Nicholas took was to attach a conventional parachute to his body as well, in case Leonardo's was a disaster.

"ognuno si potrà gettare da qualsiasi altezza senza alcun rischio" ANYONE CAN JUMP FROM NO matter what height without any risk whatsoever

In July 2000, Nicholas jumped off a hot air balloon at 3,000 meters and floated gracefully through the skies of South Africa for almost 10 minutes. He stated that Leonardo's parachute gave a smooth ride—smoother than modern parachutes—and that it felt as though he was floating through space. He cut himself free from Leonardo's parachute about 2,000 feet above the ground because he was afraid that the weight of the parachute would injure him upon landing He then used a modern parachute with a ripcord, which gave him a very safe landing.

History of the Modern Parachute

The term parachute *was coined by Sebastian Lenormand in France in 1783, and though he claims to have invented it, Lenormand apparently never tried the parachute out. A couple of years later a man named Jean Pierre Blanchard built and tested a parachute. First he launched a dog from a hot air balloon. Luckily for the dog, the parachute worked. Later, Blanchard used his parachute to save his own life: his hot air balloon malfunctioned when he used his parachute to safely reach the ground.*

While the first parachutes were made of linen and wood (similar to Leonardo's design), parachute innovators quickly turned to lighter and more compactable materials such as silk. In 1797 a man named Andrew Garnerin tested a silk parachute successfully, and silk became the material of choice in parachute construction. Garnerin later made a vented parachute, which allowed for more stability and a smoother ride. In 1890, two men named Paul Letterman and Katchen Paulus invented the first knapsack parachute. This allowed for an easier launch—the parachute was now confined to a small backpack rather than floating loose.

In 1912, U.S. Army Captain Albert Berry made the very first jump from an airplane and parachuted through the air over Missouri. Today, modern parachutes use "ram-air," or parafoil wings that self-inflate by trapping air between two layers of material and allow for complete control of direction. Parachutes are generally safe, as long as certain precautions are taken (such as packing them correctly). Although it's not common, parachutes can malfunction. Backup parachutes have been designed so that the jumper has a reliable safety mechanism.

Make Leonardo's Parachute

What you'll need
- four 8½-by-11-inch pieces of paper
- pencil
- ruler
- scissors
- markers/decorations/glue (optional)
- tape (Scotch tape will work best)
- dental floss or fishing line
- a small weight like a bolt, washers, or an action figure

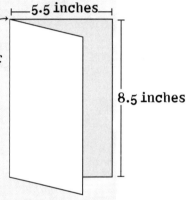

What to do

1 Take one of the pieces of paper and fold it in half, widthwise. Use your pencil to mark the middle of the page. Unfold it. Using your ruler, draw a straight line from the middle mark to the bottom corners of the paper. It will make a triangle.

2 Do the same with the other three pieces of paper.

3 Now cut out all four triangles.

4 If you would like to decorate your triangles, now is the time to do it. Remember that only one side of the parachute will be seen.

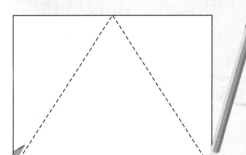

Cut out triangles

5 Place a piece of tape along one side of one triangle lengthwise so that half the tape is on the triangle and the other half is ready to be taped to something

Tape along edges

Tape along edges

Tape along edges

else. Take another triangle, line one side up with the first triangle. Use the tape to attach the two triangles. Repeat this until you have all four triangles taped together.

6 Make a crease on each seam of tape. This should form the triangles into a pyramid, with the points of the triangles meeting at the top. Tape the last seam together, so that you have a sturdy pyramid.

7 Next, cut four equal pieces of dental floss, about 12 inches long. Tape one piece to each corner of your parachute. Tie your weight to the floss, making sure each string stays approximately the same length (this will allow for a smoother flight).

8 Test your parachute by throwing it off a balcony or out a window and watch it glide. You can try all sorts of variations: shorten or lengthen the string, cut a small hole in the top of the parachute, get a heavier or lighter weight, and so on.

Tape 4th side together to form pyramid

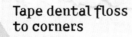

Tape dental floss to corners

You now have a Leonardo parachute replica.

Washer(s) used as weight

Leonardo's Anemometer

Leonardo's interest in flying also led to his fascination with the air itself. In his observations of different kinds of birds and their ability to fly, he noticed that all birds, whether they were as small as finches or as large as eagles and vultures, were able to get airborne and soar and rise on air currents equally well. These observations led Leonardo to believe that the wind followed laws similar to those of water, and if he could understand how wind and air swirled and pooled in the sky, he could figure out how to fly.

Leonardo drew many designs for machines that would measure the "quality and thickness of the air," including devices that measured air humidity and the flow of air over different surfaces. One of these devices was a mechanical anemometer, which is a machine for measuring windspeed. In one of his notebooks Leonardo drew a simple lever anemometer, which was a frame holding a free-swinging disk. The idea behind the anemometer was simple: when the wind blew, it would push the disk up the scale marked on the side of the frame and show, very briefly, what the force of the wind was at any given moment.

The idea of measuring windspeed didn't start with Leonardo. In fact, the first mechanical anemometer was created by another very famous Italian, Leon Battista Alberti. In 1450, a few years before Leonardo was born, Battista designed the disk anemometer that Leonardo drew many years later. But Leonardo's contribution to the study of wind-speed took Alberti's idea a bit further. Leonardo realized that simply measuring a gust of wind at any given time by looking at a mark on a scale didn't help determine the wind speed over time. So Leonardo's drawing included the notation that he would need a clock alongside the anemometer in order to accurately record the speed of the wind.

Build It Yourself

Make Your Own Anemometer

Here are two different kinds of anemometers. The first one is a replica of the mechanical anemometer designed by Leon Battista Alberti and Leonardo. This is a very easy anemometer to build to check the force of the wind at any given moment.

The second anemometer is known as a hemispherical cup anemomenter, and was invented in 1846 by an Irish researcher named John Thomas Romney Robinson. This kind of anemometer rotates with the wind, and windspeed is calculated based on its number of revolutions per minute.

Mechanical Anemometer

What you'll need

- top of a cardboard shoebox
- scissors
- permanent marker
- ruler
- tape
- playing card

What to do

1   Cut the top off the lid of the shoebox. The remaining four sides will be your anemometer frame.

2   Cut along one corner seam to open the frame. You'll have one long side free. This long side will be the gauge.

3   Measure and mark equal lengths on the gauge, and number the marks.

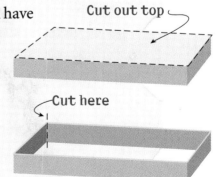

Cut out top

Cut here

4 Bend the gauge toward the other long side of the frame and tape it onto that side.

5 Tape the playing card to the top of the frame so it hangs down and can swing freely.

When a gust of wind comes, the playing card will swing up to a point on the gauge. Make a chart of the number of times the playing card reaches different points on the gauge.

Tape here

Mark equal lengths on guage

Tape here

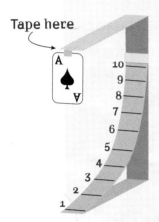

Hemispheric Cup Anemometer

What you'll need

- five 3-ounce paper cups
- nail or paper punch (to make holes in the cups)
- two straws
- stapler
- straight pin
- scissors
- pencil with an eraser

What to do

1 Punch a hole in four of the five cups approximately half an inch below the rim.

half inch

quarter inch

4 holes spaced evenly around cup

2 Punch four holes in the fifth cup. They should be spaced equally apart, a quarter of an inch below the rim. Punch another hole in the center of the bottom of the cup. This cup will be the hub for your anemometer.

3 Push a straw through the hole in one of the four cups. Fold the end of the straw and staple it to the side of the cup opposite the hole. This will keep the cup on the straw when it is turning in the wind. Repeat this step with another cup and the second straw.

Bend straw against inside edge of cup and staple it in place

(Looking down into the cup)

4 Take one of the straw and cup pieces and push the free end of the straw through opposite holes in the hub cup (the fifth cup with the four holes in it). When the straw has come through the hub cup, push another cup onto the end. Make sure the opening of this cup is facing in the opposite direction of the cup on the other end of

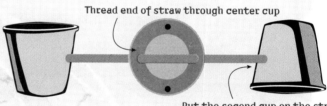

Thread end of straw through center cup

Put the second cup on the straw and staple it in place like the first one

the straw. Fold the end of the straw and staple it. Repeat this with the last cup.

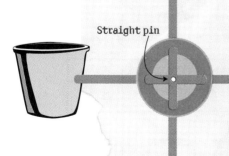

Straight pin

5 Take the straight pin and push it through the straws where they intersect. Push the eraser end of the pencil up through the hole in the bottom of the cup as far as it will go, pushing the pin into the eraser. The pin will hold your anemometer together. Your anemometer is ready to go!

(Looking into cup)

(Looking at the bottom)

Insert pencil through hole in the bottom of the center cup and push eraser onto the pin inserted in the top

How to use your anemometer

To calculate the velocity of your anemometer's rotation, count the number of revolutions your anemometer makes in one minute. Then measure the circumference (in feet) of the circle your anemometer makes. Remember that the formula for figuring out the circumference of a circle is to measure the diameter of the circle by π, which is 3.14. Multiply the revolutions per minute you recorded with the circumference of the circle and you'll have a rough estimate of the velocity of your anemometer 's rotation (and an even rougher estimate of the windspeed—your anemometer doesn't take into account factors like friction or drag).

The Beaufort Scale

Say you take out your anemometers (both the mechanical and hemispheric cup models), and both of them blow right out of your hands. You don't need an anemometer to know it's a very windy day. But just how windy? The Beaufort Scale is a numbered scale that measures windspeed, and it uses observation of things like trees and smoke to determine windspeed. The higher the number on the Beaufort Scale, the greater the wind speed.

Beaufort number	description of wind	possible effects of the wind	wind speed km/hour
0	calm	smoke rises vertically	0–2
1	light air	direction of wind shown by smoke	3–5
2	light breeze	wind felt on face	6–11
3	gentle breeze	the wind extends a small flag	12–19
4	moderate breeze	loose paper is moved	20–29
5	fresh breeze	small trees begin to sway	30–39
6	strong breeze	umbrellas are difficult to hold	40–50
7	moderate gale the wind	difficult to walk against	51–61
8	fresh gale	twigs break off trees	62–74
9	strong gale are removed	chimney pots and slates	75–86
10	whole gale	trees uprooted	87–101
11	violent storm communications	widespread damage to buildings and woodlands	102–120
12	hurricane	devastation occurs	over 121

Leonardo's War Inventions

Virtually every account of Leonardo's life talks about his love of animals, his gentle nature, and his dislike of violence. So why were so many of his inventions based on warfare? Part of the reason has to do with the time in which he lived. The Renaissance was a time of great change and new ideas in the arts, in science, and even in religion, but it was also a time of unease and instability, especially when it came to politics and power.

During the Renaissance, Italy wasn't ruled by a single king or queen, as England and France were. Instead, it was divided into lots of independent city-states, tiny kingdoms, duchies, and republics, all ruled by different people and governments. The southernmost part of Italy, called Naples, was ruled by a king. Central Italy was ruled by the Church, headed by the Pope. The northern half of the country was divided into city-states, which were independent regions centered on major cities. Some of these city-states were ruled by dukes (*duchy* literally means a region ruled by a duke), and others were ruled by families who came to power—and hung on to it—by spending lots and lots of money.

Map of Italy during Leonardo's time.

Rulers of each city-state could only stay in power as long as they could keep the leaders of other city-states from taking over their territories. They were constantly feuding, making and breaking secret alliances with each other, and often engaging in outright warfare. As a result, many of the cities were almost like fortresses.

Some, such as Florence and Siena, were surrounded by high walls to defend against attackers. In some cities, individuals even built their homes with high towers they could escape to and defend themselves from in case of attack by enemies. Rulers of these city-states wanted any strategic military advantage they could find.

Leonardo realized that his fascination with machines and how they worked could not only be applied to flight, or to making everyday machines work more efficiently, but also to waging war. He knew his talents could make him a useful and valuable asset to the leaders of these city-states. So in 1482, he wrote a letter to Ludovico Sforza, the ruler of Milan, presenting himself as a military engineer. In his letter Leonardo outlined all of the remarkable weapons, bridges, and fortifications he could create to keep Milan safe from outside attack. Leonardo's letter so impressed Sforza that he was immediately invited to Milan, where he worked for the Sforza family for the next 17 years.

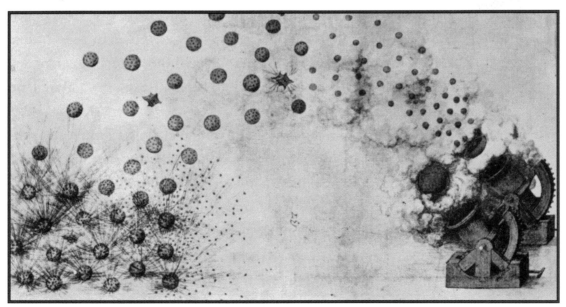

Sketch for a cannon with exploding cannon balls.

Most of the weapons and inventions Leonardo proposed to Sforza were never built, and in fact, some of them wouldn't really have worked if he had tried to create them. But consider this: the diagrams and drawings of weapons, fortifications, and military machines that Leonardo made in his notebooks show the beginnings of inventions that are used every day today, in both military and civilian life, including the life preserver, the step ladder, armored vehicles, and temporary bridges.

Excerpts of Letter from Leonardo to Ludovico Sforza

Ludovico Sforza

"Most Illustrious Lord: Having now sufficiently seen and considered the proofs of all those who proclaim themselves masters and inventors of instruments of war, and finding that their invention and use of the said instruments are nothing different from common practice, I am emboldened, without prejudice to any one else, to put myself in communications with Your Excellency, in order to acquaint you with my secrets, thereafter offering myself at your pleasure effectually to demonstrate at opportune times all those things which are in part briefly noted below:

I have a sort of extremely light and strong bridges, adapted to be most easily carried, and with them you may pursue, and at any time flee from the enemy.

I have kinds of mortars, most convenient and easy to carry, and with these can fling small stones almost resembling a storm; and with the smoke of these causing great terror to the enemy, to his great detriment and confusion.

I will make covered chariots, safe and unattackable, which, entering among the enemy with their artillery, there is no body of men so great but they would break them.

In case of need I will make big guns, mortars, and light ordnance of fine and useful forms, out of the common type. Where the operation of bombardment should fail, I would contrive catapults, mangonels, trabocchi [trebuchet] and other machines of marvelous efficacy and not in common use.

In short, I can contrive various and endless means of offence and defense."

trebuchet—hurls heavy stones

Leonardo's Safety Bridge

Jn his famous letter to Ludovico Sforza, Leonardo said that he had "a sort of extremely light and strong bridges, adapted to be most easily carried." Leonardo had designed several temporary bridges that could be put together and taken apart fairly quickly and easily. One of the most interesting is his "safety bridge." In one of his notebooks, Leonardo described this bridge as "a safety bridge, made by an army out of necessity, from plants, which they find at the river banks. And this is the framework of this bridge, that is the building skeleton which then will be covered with thicker wood and then with branches of trees—and brooms and sods. And the more it is loaded, the more it tightens."

Remember Leonardo's bridge that we talked about on page 9? It was never built, and the drawings Leonardo made for it sat unused for 400 years. But in 1996, a Norwegian artist saw a model of the bridge and convinced the Norwegian government to build a wooden version for pedestrians just outside of Oslo, the Norwegian capital. The world's first Leonardo Bridge officially opened in 2001.

World's first Leonardo Bridge in Oslo, Norway.

Build It Yourself

Make Your Own Portable Bridge

You can build a model of this bridge to be any size, from a tiny Popsicle stick table-top model, to a full-size version made from tree branches and brush. For a full-size bridge you will need to lash the ladder components together with rope. If you make the table-top version you won't need glue or anything to hold the bridge components together: The amazing thing about Leonardo's bridge is that the supports are "woven" into a grid that makes the bridge sturdier as more weight is put on it.

The directions below are for building a full-size version of the bridge using branches from around your yard (or from a local park). Don't build it over water, and make absolutely sure that no one is underneath the bridge when you are constructing it or trying it out!

What you'll need

- six sticks approximately 3 feet long for sides of the ladder (or any size as long as they are all about the same length)
- five sticks approximately 1 foot long for the ladder rungs (about a third as long as the ladder sides)
- ten pieces of rope or string to lash cross-pieces to ladder sides
- brush or cardboard to lay over the framework

What to do

1 Place the first two 3-foot long sticks on the ground lengthwise. Measure up approximately 1 foot, and lash one of the 1-foot rungs to the sticks as shown (diagram at left).

2 Measure up another foot and do the same thing.

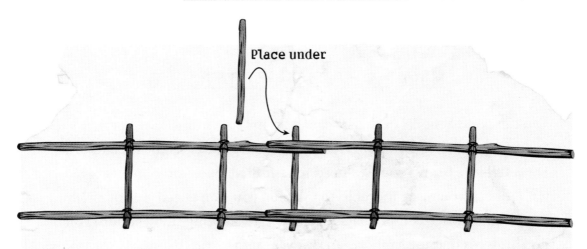

Place under

3 Now lay out two more 3-foot-long sticks and follow the directions as above.

4 You will now have two mini-ladders. Lay these on the ground end to end, making sure that the last foot of each mini ladder is overlapping. Take the last foot-long ladder rung and place it under the two long ladder pieces.

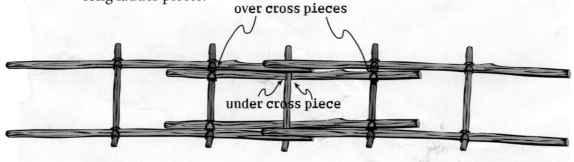

over cross pieces

under cross piece

5 Take the last two 3-foot ladder pieces and place one end of each on top of the last ladder rung on one side, under the center ladder rung, and back on top of the top ladder rung on the other side. This will make the bridge arc. Lash the ends of the long pieces to the rungs.

6 Lay brush, boughs, and whatever else you have to cover the framework and make your bridge support more weight. If you don't have brush you can always use large pieces of cardboard or even blankets (be careful you don't fall through!)

Leonardo's Trebuchet

Leonardo really wasn't very experienced in warfare or weaponry, but he loved a challenge, and engineers, especially military engineers, were valued much more highly than regular artists—even painters with the talents of Leonardo. Why were they so valued? Because unlike artists, who could only create beautiful things to celebrate a ruler, a military engineer could actually keep that ruler in power. When Leonardo wrote his letter to Ludovico Sforza, Italy was a pretty dangerous place: rulers were only as powerful as their latest political deal or military victory, so while they wanted beautiful paintings and lovely artwork, they needed military victories and political strength to make sure they stayed in power long enough to enjoy them.

Milan, the city Sforza ruled, was known for its weaponry. It was famous for its armorers' shops, which made swords, helmets, shields, and other traditional weapons that were sold all over the world. But what Milan didn't have was the kind of exotic weapons Leonardo proposed, weapons that would help make Milan, and its ruler,

Horse-drawn weapon.

Sforza, a military power like the Turks to the east and the European kingdoms to the north. Leonardo suggested to Sforza that he could make siege weapons such as mines, cannon balls, armored tanks, catapults, and trebuchets, and other machines that would allow the Italians to attack their enemies and fight in pitched battles.

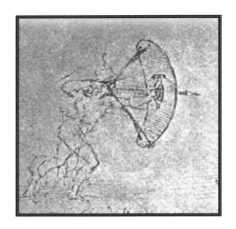

Leonardo's drawings for catapults, giant crossbows, slingshots, and other war inventions weren't totally his own ideas—these weapons had been in use for hundreds of years, and some had been used for thousands of years. The catapult, for example, had been around since the time of the ancient Greeks. Most of Leonardo's inventions and innovations were created to omit one important element: humans. In almost every case, his machines were designed to work with as little manpower as possible. His ideas also focused on making machines as efficient as possible, by designing one machine to several tasks. Leonardo designed a multiple-barreled machine gun that was arranged almost like an organ on wheels. Eleven of the barrels would fire, then the carriage would move forward, and another set of barrels would move into place and fire again. Leonardo modernized the crossbow by making it almost complely automated. One person would turn a crank, which would both fire the crossbow and reload the arrows one after another.

Exploding artillery shell.

Build It Yourself

Make Your Own Trebuchet

A trebuchet was a kind of catapult with a basket on one end that acted as a counterweight. The launcher was pulled back and secured, loaded with boulders or other heavy objects, and then the counterweight basket was filled with ballast. When the launcher was set loose, the counterweight would swing down with great force, sending the launching arm (and its rocks) flying in an arc. This trebuchet is a version of an ancient model that Leonardo designed for the duke of Milan.

What you'll need
- six pieces of wood approximately 1 foot long and 1–2 inches wide
- wood glue or hammer and small nails
- ruler
- piece of wood approximately 8 inches long and 1–2 inches wide
- dowel rod ⅝ inch or smaller in diameter, 18 inches long
- drill with a bit one size larger than the diameter of the dowel rod
- pint-size milk carton
- bag tie—plastic ones for trash bags work great
- scissors
- duct tape
- measuring cup—½ cup size works well
- weights and projectiles: small stones, pennies, washers, etc.

What to do

1 To build your frame, either nail or glue four of the pieces of scrap wood to form a square.

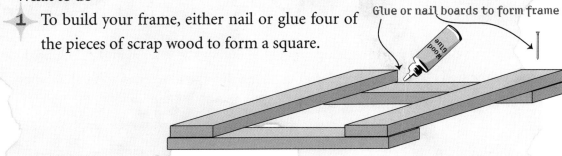

Glue or nail boards to form frame

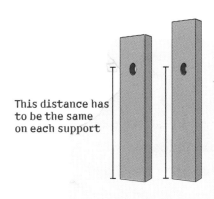

This distance has to be the same on each support

2 Take two more pieces of wood that are approximately the same height. These will be the supports for the swinging arm of your trebuchet, so while the supports don't have to be exactly the same height, the holes you drill in them must be at exactly the same height or the dowel rod won't rotate freely. Measure 7 or 8 inches from the bottom of the supports and drill a hole through each one that is slightly larger than the diameter of the dowel rod.

3 Glue or nail the supports to the frame.

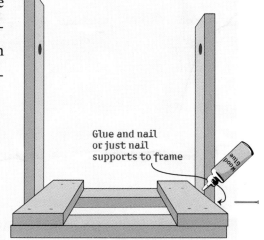

Glue and nail or just nail supports to frame

Wood glue

Drill hole

Drill hole to attach weight basket

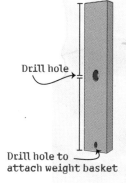

4 Drill a hole slightly wider than the diameter of the dowel halfway down the final, and shorter, piece of wood and also about an inch from one end. This will be the lever arm of your trebuchet, and must be able to swing freely on the dowel, so make sure you have plenty of clearance on both the top and bottom before you drill. You might need some parental supervision.

5 The hole at the end of the lever arm is for your weight basket. You'll thread a bag tie through this hole so make sure it is wide enough for a bag tie to fit.

6 Tape or glue the measuring cup to the end of the lever arm (the end without the hole), making sure that it can clear both ends of the trebuchet when swung.

Thread bag tie through holes in the milk carton and the hole in the arm

Tape measuring cup to arm

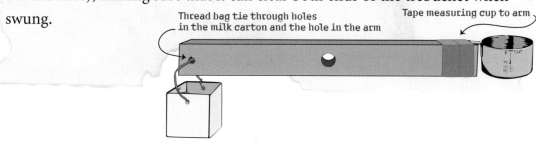

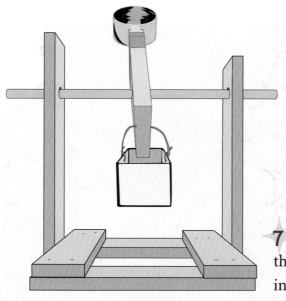

7 Make the weight basket by cutting the pint milk carton in half. Poke a hole in both sides, and thread the bag tie through one of them. Thread the bag tie through the lever arm and then through the other hole in the milk carton. Attach the bag tie to itself so the weight basket is securely on the lever arm.

8 Slide the dowel through one of the frame supports, slide the lever arm onto the dowel, and then slide the dowel onto the trebuchet frame.

9 Fill the weight basket with small stones, metal washers, or anything to give it some weight.

10 Load the measuring cup with your projectiles—marbles or small stones work great. Pull the measuring cup down, then let go—the weight in the weight basket will swing down and launch the projectiles from the measuring cup.

Leonardo's Tank

When Leonardo wrote to Ludovico Sforza and told him that he could "make covered chariots, safe and unattackable," he was designing a war weapon that other engineers of his time were experimenting with, too. Most of these weapons and other tanks were designed to be powered by sail, but Leonardo's covered chariot was designed to be used as an assault vehicle in battle, powered by cranks. The sides of the "chariot," or tank, were wood covered with metal plates and had sloping surfaces to deflect arrows, cannon and artillery balls, and spears. The "lid" of the tank made it possible for soldiers to have a 360-degree view of their enemy, and small openings in the lower part of the tank around the front and back were for long lances that could impale horses and their riders who got in the way. Leonardo designed his covered chariot to go forward and backward by cranking a handle that would turn the wheels. Originally he had proposed that horses power the tank by walking around a crankshaft, but decided against it because he thought they would become hard to manage in a small space.

Leonardo's tank.

Build It Yourself

Make Your Own Armored Tank

This project has a lot of steps, but all of them are easy. In the end you'll have a pretty good replica of Leonardo's tank that can move on its own. This project requires that you use a drill with a 1¼ inch drill bit for one part, so you may need a little help from your parents.

What you'll need
- large kitchen-size match box (about 5 inches long by 2½ inches wide)
- measuring tape or ruler
- pencil
- Xacto knife
- scissors
- two 4½-inch-long, ¼-inch-diameter dowel rods
- two large (3½-inch) rubber bands
- duct tape
- glue
- tweezers or a paper clip
- toothpicks
- four 3¼-inch yogurt lids—standard 1-cup size
- 12-by-12-inch piece of heavy cardboard or balsa wood
- mechanical compass for making circles
- 6–11 wooden skewers or long matchsticks for spears
- 9½-inch aluminum pie plate
- 9¼-inch round aluminum casserole pan (deeper than the pie plate)
- ¼-inch bit and a drill (optional but handy) or large nail
- piece of posterboard
- piece of string 11 inches long
- stapler
- tin foil

What to do

Part 1: Make the chassis and "motor"

1 Take the matchbox and measure ¾ inch from each long end. Cut two rectangles about 1 inch wide by 1½ inches long. These will be the openings you'll use to insert the axles and rubber band drive mechanism.

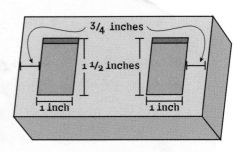

2 Turn the box on its side. Measure ½ inch from each end and ½ inch from the bottom on both sides. Poke (or drill) a hole straight through the matchbox so you have matching holes on both sides. This is where you'll put the dowel rods for the wheel axles, so measure carefully.

½ inch in, ½ inch up from bottom

3 Wrap one of the rubber bands around one of the dowels as shown, approximately two-thirds of the way from one end. Pull to make it really tight, then wrap duct tape around the knot and dot some glue on it. You want to make sure the rubber band can't slip around on the dowel. Do the same thing for the second dowel.

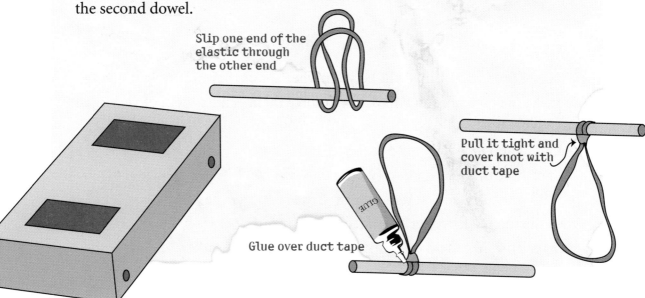

Slip one end of the elastic through the other end

Pull it tight and cover knot with duct tape

Glue over duct tape

4 Stick the dowels into the axle holes by putting the end opposite the elastic into the big hole in the top of the box and far into the wheel axle hole, then wiggling the other end through into the opposite hole.

5 Poke a hole in each end of the matchbox so you can fish out the rubber band with a pair of tweezers or a bent paper clip. The rubber band will stretch and put tension on the axles. Stick a piece of skewer or matchstick in the end of the rubber band so it won't slip back into the hole, then tape over it so it's secure.

Pull elastic out through the hole in the opposite end and secure with little stick

Glue cardboard inserts into yogurt lids and drill holes in center

6 The four yogurt lids will be your wheels, but they aren't rigid enough to make the tank go. You'll have to reinforce them. Take a piece of very rigid cardboard (or balsa wood if you have it) and draw four 3-inch circles. Cut them out and glue them into the yogurt lids. When the glue has dried, drill a ¼-inch hole through the center of each one. The little molded tip in the yogurt lid is the center. Use that as your guide. Now put the wheels on the axles with the top of the yogurt lids facing (cardboard liners facing out) to make sure they fit. Take them off again, and put glue into the hole you drilled, then

carefully put the wheels back on and let the glue dry. You now have your motor and chassis!

7 Center the matchbox chassis in the bottom of the casserole pan. Mark on the bottom of the pan where the matchbox is and where the outside edges of the wheels sit— you're going to cut rectangles in the bottom of the pan for the wheels to go through, so mark them carefully. The marks should be about ¾-inch wide and 3½ inches long for each wheel. Cut out the four rectancles and put the matchbox chassis in to see if the wheels fit through. Expand the slots if necessary so the wheels can move without scraping the pan. Take out the matchbox chassis and set it aside. You can duct tape the edges of the slots if they are sharp.

Draw around the matchbox chassis and cut out slots for wheels

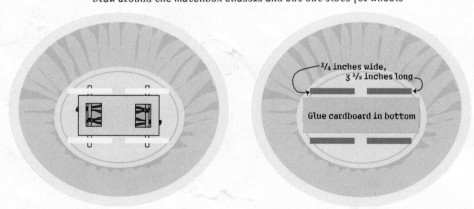

8 Depending on the stiffness of the aluminum casserole pan you're using, you might want to reinforce the bottom a bit so it doesn't crumple when you're pushing the tank. Cut out a cardboard rectangle about 2½ inches wide by 7 inches long. Tape or glue it to the bottom of the pan. Then glue the matchbox chassis into the bottom of the pan. While the glue dries you'll need to support the casserole pan on something (two books, one on each side of the casserole pan, work well) so the wheels can come out the bottom and the

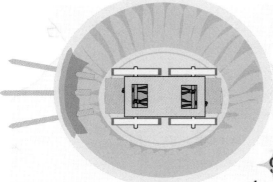

matchbox rests securely on the bottom of the pan. When the glue dries, reinforce it by duct taping the matchbox to the bottom, too.

9 Finally, poke three or four holes in the front of the pan. Take three of the long matchsticks and break them in half, then push them through the holes. These are the long lances that would impale enemy horses as the tank moved forward. Tape the sticks to the inside of the pan. The bottom of your tank is ready to go!

Part 2: Make the dome

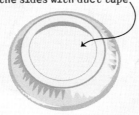

Cut the bottom out of pie plate leaving about a 1-inch rim and cover the sides with duct tape

1 Cut out the bottom of the pie plate, leaving about an inch of the bottom as a rim. Duct tape the entire thing for armour plating, if you like.

2 Lay out the piece of posterboard. Using the 11-inch piece of string, swing an arc from one edge of the poster board to the other. You'll have a half-circle 22 inches in diameter. Cut the string to a length of 7 inches and swing another arc inside the first half-circle (see diagram).

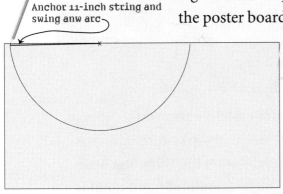

Anchor 11-inch string and swing anw arc

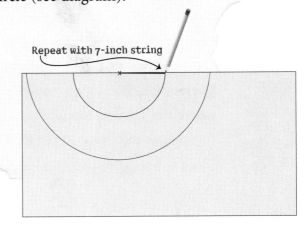

Repeat with 7-inch string

3 Cut out the arc and roll the ends together so it fits over the pie plate. Mark where the ends overlap. This is where you'll

Cut off excess

staple them together later. Cut off the excess overlap, making sure you leave enough extra to staple the ends together.

Mark where ends overlap

Pie plate

4 Cut or break six of the long match sticks so the pieces are approximately 5 inches long. Lay them out evenly in a fan shape on the posterboard arc, with their ends touching. Leave a couple of inches of poster-board on either side. Glue the matchsticks onto the posterboard.

Lay matchsticks as instructed and glue to posterboard

5 When the glue is dry, roll up the half circle and fit it back onto the pie plate. Tape or staple the ends together. You can cover the dome in duct tape or tin foil for armor, if you like.

6 To make the turret, draw a 5½-inch diameter circle on the remaining poster board and cut it out. Cut a line from one edge to the center of the circle. Now roll the posterboard circle until it fits on top of the dome sticks. You can make it wider or narrower depending on how tightly you roll it to-gether. When you get it the size you want, staple or tape the sides together. There should be a gap between the dome of the tank and the turret: that's where the soldiers would stand to shoot at their enemies. You can cover the turret with duct tape or tin foil before gluing it onto the sticks.

cut

5½ inch circle

7 When the glue is dry, place the dome on the bottom of the tank, and duct tape them together. Put your tank on a flat surface. Roll it backward; the rubber bands will wind on the wheel axles. When you release the tank, it will move forward on its own.

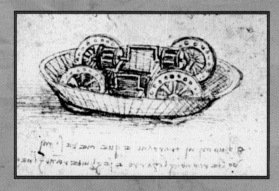

Leonardo's Tank Flaw

Leonardo's tank design had one major problem: the front and rear wheels he drew would have turned in opposite directions, meaning it would have been impossible to drive the tank. Historians have wondered if this was on purpose, either so other people wouldn't steal his idea, or because in his heart, Leonardo was a pacifist and hated war. On the other hand, it could just have been a mistake. What do you think?

Image Credits

page 1, Self portrait. Red chalk drawing. Scala/Art Resource, NY; Biblioteca Reale, Turin, Italy.

page 2, Weapons. Courtesy of Planet Art.

page 2, Flying machine. Snark/Art Resource, NY; Biblioteca Ambrosiana, Milan, Italy.

page 2, *Vitruvian Man,* ca.1492. Drawing. Scala/Art Resource, NY; Accademia, Venice, Italy.

page 8, From *The Last Supper.* Leonardo da Vinci, Adolpf Rosenberg, 1903.

page 9, *The Bridge of the Golden Horn.* Courtesy Leonardo Bridge Project.

page 11, *Mona Lisa,* 1503–1506. Oil on wood. Erich Lessing/Art Resource, NY; Louvre, Paris, France.

page 12, Portrait of Andrea Verrocchio by Lorenzo di Credi, 1459–1537. Alinari/Art Resource, NY; Uffizi, Florence, Italy.

page 12, *The Baptisim of Christ,* Verrocchio. Painted in collaberation with his pupils, Leonardo da Vinci & Lorenzo di Credi. Erich Lessing/Art Resource, NY; Uffizi, Florence, Italy.

page 13, Caricatures. *Leonardo da Vinci,* Adolpf Rosenberg, 1903.

page 13, *Vitruvian Man,* ca.1492. Drawing. Scala/Art Resource, NY; Accademia, Venice, Italy.

page 15, From *The Baptism of Christ,* after a photograph from the original by G. Brogi, Florence, *Leonardo da Vinci.* Adolf Rosenberg, 1903.

page 23, Masks. Courtesy of Planet Art.

page 24, Costumes. Alinari/Art Resources, NY.

page 27, From *The Last Supper. Leonardo da Vinci,* Adolpf Rosenberg, 1903.

page 33, Parabolic compass. Courtesy of Planet Art.

page 37, Dragon. Courtesy of Planet Art.

page 38, Rebus. Courtesy of Planet Art.

page 59, Hygrometer. Courtesy of Planet Art.

page 66, Archimedes screw and water wheel, from the Codex Atlanticus. Art Resource, NY; Biblioteca Ambrosiana, Milan, Italy.

page 67, Canel with locks, from the Codex Atlanticus. Art Resource, NY; Biblioteca Ambrosiana, Milan, Italy.

page 68, Dredging machine. Courtesy of Planet Art.

page 78, Birds in flight. Courtesy of Planet Art.

page 78, Flying machine. Ms.B, fol. 74 verso, detail. Art Resource, NY; Bibliotheque de L'Institut de France, Paris, France.

page 83, Helical Air Screw. Ms. B, fol. 83 verso. Art Resource, NY; Bibliotheque de L'Institut de France, Paris, France.

page 88, Parachute. Courtesy of Planet Art.

page 98, Cannons, from the Codex Atlanticus, fol. 9v. Art Resource, NY; Bibliotheque de L'Institut de France, Paris, France.

page 100, Leonardo Bridge, Oslo, Norway. Terje Johansen.

page 103, Drawing of chariots. Courtesy of Planet Art.

page 104, Drawings. *Leonardo da Vinci,* Adolf Rosenberg, 1903.

pages 108 and 115, Drawing of tanks. Art Resource, NY; British Museum, London, Great Britain.

Glossary

acidic: a substance with a high acid content, characterized by a sour taste.

algebra: math using letters as symbols.

anatomy: the study of the physical structure of plants, animals, insects, and people.

ancient Greece: the Greek-speaking world from about 1600 BCE to about 130 BCE.

ancient Rome: the period from about 750 BCE to about 400 CE, when Rome grew from a tiny town to a huge empire.

anemometer: an instrument that measures wind speed.

apprentice: someone who is learning an art (such as sculpting or painting), or a trade (such as architecture or shoemaking) from a master.

arithmetic: using numbers to calculate.

basic: a substance with a high base content, characterized by a bitter taste.

bellows: a device that can be expanded to draw air in and compressed to force the air out.

Before Common Era, BCE: all the years before Jesus Christ was born. Also known as BC.

biblical flood: a flood mentioned in the bible; a major flood.

Black Death: a disease that killed over 50 million people throughout Asia and Europe in the fourteenth century.

bottega: the Italian word for artist's studio.

bubonic plague: see Black Death.

butchering: slaughtering and preparing the meat of an animal for food.

camera obscura: a box or small darkened room with a small hole through which an image of what is outside is projected inside on one of the sides.

canal: an artificial waterway constructed for shipping or irrigation.

catapult: a large war machine used to hurl stones at an enemy.

chassis: the frame and wheels that support the engine and body of a motor vehicle.

chiaroscuro: the use of light and shade in paintings to make figures look three-dimensional.

Common Era, CE: all the years after Jesus Christ was born. Also known as AD.

density: how thick, compact, or hard something is.

ducat: money from Venice, Italy, during Leonardo's time.

Duomo of Santa Maria del Fiore: a church in Florence, Italy.

dyeing: coloring or staining something, like fabric or hair.

erosion: the gradual destruction, reduction, or weakening of something by aging, water, wind, ice, or chemicals.

feudal: the social system in Europe in the Middle Ages in which peasants or slaves farmed land owned by nobles.

Flemish: from Flanders, a region that combines western Belgium and part of France.

florin: coins from Florence, Italy, during Leonardo's time.

fossils: a remnant or trace of a formerly living thing that has died.

friction: the rubbing of two objects when one or both are moving and the resistance to one or both of these objects that results from their contact.

geometry: the properties and relationships of points, lines, angles, curves, surfaces, and solids.

horizon: straight ahead, where the sky meets the earth.

hydrometer: a device that measures the density of liquids.

hygrometer: a device that measures the humidity in the air.

icosahedron: a 20-faced figure.

intarsia: gluing different colors of wood together in complicated patterns.

linear perspective: drawings or paintings are given apparent depth by showing parallel lines as converging on the horizon.

lock: an enclosure in a canal with gates at each end used in raising or lowering boats as they pass from one level to another.

Ludovico Sforza: the duke of Milan, Leonardo's first and longest patron.

Medici family: patrons of the arts during the Renaissance.

merchant: a businessman, like a storeowner or trader.

meteorology: the study of climate and weather.

Middle Ages: the period in European history between the end of the Roman Empire in the fifth century (400s), and the late fourteenth century (late 1300s).

middle class: a class of people during the Renaissance who valued education and had enough money for luxuries.

Modern Age: present or recent times, also known as modern era.

noble: a wealthy and often powerful landowner.

octahedron: an 8-faced figure.

optics: the science of light and sight.

ornithopter: an early flying machine that operated using flapping wings.

orthogonals: lines that come together at the same vanishing point.

patron: someone who supports an event, institution, or person.

peasant: a poor farmer who does not own their land.

perspective: a method of graphically depicting three-dimensional objects and spatial relationships to a two-dimensional plane.

perspectograph: an instrument used by painters for transferring the points and outlines of an object in correct proportions.

pistils: the female reproductive part of a flower.

pitched battle: a fierce battle fought by opponents who have taken up positions close to one another.

polygon: a many-sided figure.

polyhedra: the plural of polyhedron.

polyhedron: a three-dimensional polygon.

rebus: a representation of words in the form of pictures or symbols, often as a puzzle.

Renaissance: the period in European history from about the late 1300s through the 1500s. It marked the end of the Middle Ages and brought new life to society and appreciation for the arts.

replica: an accurate copy of something.

revolutions: complete, circular turns.

rhombicuboctahedron: a 26-faced figure.

saffron: a deep yellow-orange color.

sfumato: the gradual blending or blurring of one area of color into another without a sharp outline.

Straits of Bosphorus: the body of water separating Europe from Asia.

tanning: the process of turning animal skins and hides into leather.

trebuchet: a medieval catapult for hurling heavy stones.

vanishing point: a point in a drawing or painting where lines seem to meet or where something disappears.

velocity: speed, or a measure of speed.

Venetian: from Venice.

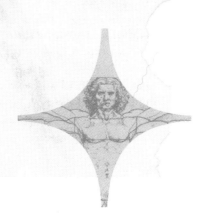

Bibliography/Resources

Books and Articles

Bramly, Serge. *Leonardo: Discovering the Life of Leonardo da Vinci*. Harper Collins, 1991.

Byrd, Robert. *Leonardo: Beautiful Dreamer*. Dutton Children's Books, New York, 2003.

Cooper, Margaret. *The Inventions of Leonardo da Vinci*. The MacMillan Company, New York, 1965.

da Vinci, Leonardo. *Prophecies and other Literary Writings*. Hesperus Press, London, 2002.

Herbert, Janis. *Leonardo da Vinci for Kids: His Life and Ideas*. Chicago Review Press, 1998.

Leoni, Maria Teresa Zanobini. *Leonardo da Vinci. Great Artists*. Enchanted Lion Books, 2003.

Lorenzi, Rossella. "Da Vinci Invented Natural Plastics." *Discovery News*, Discovery Channel Online, February 4, 2004.

McCurdy, Edward. *Leonardo da Vinci Note-Books*. Empire State Book Company, New York, 1923.

McLanahan, Richard. *Leonardo da Vinci*. First Impression, Introductions to Art. Harry N. Abrams, New York, 1990.

Nicholl, Charles. *Leonardo da Vinci: Flights of the Mind*. Viking, 2004.

Nuland, Sherwin. *Leonardo da Vinci*. Penguin Lives, Penguin Putnam, New York, 2000.

Raboff, Ernest. *Leonardo da Vinci*. Art for Children series, Doubleday & Company, Garden City, New York, 1987.

Richter, Jean Paul. *The Notebooks of Leonardo da Vinci*. Volumes I and II. Dover Publications, New York. 1970.

Ripley, Elizabeth. *Leonardo da Vinci.* Oxford University Press, 1952.

Santi, Bruno. *Leonardo.* Scala Guides to Art. Scala Publishing, Florence, 1975.

Stanley, Diane. *Leonardo da Vinci.* Morrow Junior Books, New York, 1996.

Wallace, Robert. *The World of Leonardo.* Time-Life Library of Art, Time-Life Books, New York, 1966.

Williams, Jay. *Leonardo da Vinci.* Horizon Caravel Books, Harper & Row Publishers, 1965.

Zollner, Frank and Nathan, Johannes. *Leonardo Da Vinci: The Complete Paintings and Drawings* Taschen, 2003

Web Sites

www.amnh.org/exhibitions/codex. The American Museum of Natural History had an exhibit of Bill Gates' Codex Leicester

www.cyclepublishing.com/history/leonardo

www.lairweb.org.nz/leonardo

www.lib.stevens-tech.edu/collections/davinci. This is a comprehensive online archive of works by and about Leonardo, collected and maintained by Stevens Institute of Technology.

www.museoscienza.org/english/leonardo

www.mos.org/leonardo. The Museum of Science in Boston, Massachusetts has an extensive online Leonardo exhibition, complete with experiments, activities, and quizzes.

www.museoscienza.org/english/leonardo. This is the web site of the Leonardo da Vinci National Museum of Science and Technology in Milan, Italy.

Resources for kids interested in learning more about Leonardo da Vinci

Index